Let's Play GAMES in SPANISH

a collection of games, skits, & teacher aids

Volume One
kindergarten — eighth grade

LORETTA BURKE HUBP

National Textbook Company
a division of NTC *Publishing Group* • Lincolnwood, Illinois USA

1995 Printing

Published by National Textbook Company, a division of NTC Publishing Group.
© 1985, 1980 by NTC Publishing Group, 4255 West Touhy Avenue,
Lincolnwood (Chicago), Illinois 60646-1975 U.S.A.
Manufactured in the United States of America.

4 5 6 7 8 9 ML 9 8 7 6

FOREWORD

As every teacher and student knows, foreign-language classes can be fascinating or deadly dull. *Let's Play Games in Spanish* is designed to assure that interest in foreign-language learning does not fade.

This two-volume collection features a wide variety of games, skits, and songs that can be used not only in the classroom, but at Spanish Club meetings and other get-togethers as well. Activities vary in difficulty—from the very simple to those requiring more extensive knowledge of Spanish.

Volume 1 is aimed primarily at youngsters who are just beginning their study of the language. Volume 2 was developed with older intermediate and advanced students in mind.

The games in this collection may be played by the whole class or by smaller groups of varying numbers. Each one reinforces speaking and listening skills, helping students to grow more confident and comfortable using their new language. Each activity is explained in clear, concise English to assure that students understand exactly how the games are played. The speaking parts of these activities encourage use of authentic, idiomatic Spanish.

The songs, activities, and games in the two volumes of *Let's Play Games in Spanish* all originated in Spanish-speaking countries. These books incorporate contributions of teachers and youth-group leaders from Mexico, Puerto Rico, Costa Rica, El Salvador, Peru, Chile, Uruguay, and Argentina. So, as students are learning Spanish, they will also be participating in leisure-time activities enjoyed by young people throughout the Hispanic world.

CONTENTS

I. ACTIVE GAMES

II. CLASSROOM GAMES

V. SONGS AND SINGING GAMES

I Active Games

RANA EN EL MAR

(Frog in the sea)

Any number may play.

Needed: If desired, a sign may be made showing a frog in the sea with the words: *"Rana en el mar."*

An announcer may show the sign and introduce the frog with the following words:

La rana. Está en el mar.   The frog. It is in the sea.

The frog sits on the floor, tailor fashion, and the other players form a circle around him. They move to the left and call out to him:

Rana en el mar, no   Frog in the sea. You can't
  puedes cogerme.   catch me.

The players come as close as possible to the frog without being tagged. When the frog manages to tag a player, the two change places. The frog must remain in a sitting position until she tags a player.

CARLITOS NO PUEDE COGERME

(Charley Can't Catch Me)

Here are the Spanish words for an ancient Scottish game. Any number may play.

A player, Carlitos, stands in the center of a circle formed by the other children. All clasp hands and dance around him, chanting:

Carlitos allí,	Charley there,
Carlitos aquí,	Charley here,
Carlitos no puede	Charley can't
cogerme a mí.	catch me.

The players stoop as soon as they have ended the chant. Carlitos tries to tag them before they bend down. The one who has been tagged becomes Carlitos.

PASALA

(Pass it on)

A large group of 25 to 30 may play.

Needed: A familiar Spanish song. This may be a record or the Leader may play the song on any musical instrument or sing it.

The Leader should explain that all will clap in time to the Spanish song that is being played. Whenever the music stops, the Leader touches someone and says *"Pásala"* (Pass it on). The child who has been touched must in turn touch the one to his right, repeating the *"Pásala."* The second child, as soon as he has been touched, must pass on the tag, again repeating *"Pásala,"* and so on around the circle. The last child to be touched when the music starts again comes to the center and dances while the others continue to clap to the music. The tag is repeated with each pause until the song is finished. Each additional child who comes to the center of the circle must likewise join in the dancing.

LA ORQUESTA

(The orchestra)

This game, like "Musical Chairs," may be used to practice the names of musical instruments. There must be an uneven number of players.

Needed: If desired, signs for each chair each with the name of a musical instrument. Chairs for all players except one.

All players are seated in chairs in a circle, except one who is the conductor. Each chair is labeled with the name of a musical instrument. The conductor stands in the center and raises his arms as though to conduct an orchestra. Each player pretends to play the instrument whose name is on his chair. The conductor calls the names of two musical instruments, for example, *"El clarinete y el violoncelo "* (The clarinet and the violoncello.) The two players in those chairs must exchange seats while the conductor races for one of the chairs. If the conductor is successful in getting the chair, the extra player becomes the conductor as the game continues. The new conductor repeats the names in the same manner, in pairs, or he may say:

¡*Toda la orquesta!*   The entire orchestra.

At this command, everyone in the orchestra must change places, with the conductor again trying to sit down in one of the chairs.

¿QUE NUMERO TIENE?

(What number do you have?)

Any number may play this game, an excellent one for learning Spanish numbers.

Needed: A large ball.

The players form a circle and each one is assigned a number. The Leader, in the center of the circle, calls out a number, such as *cinco* (five), and tosses the ball to the child who has that number. The child, as he catches the ball, must repeat his number. He must then call another number and toss the ball across the circle to the child who has that number. The second child repeats the action of the first, remembering to repeat his own number before he calls the next one, and the game continues in this manner.

¿CUANTAS VECES?

(How many times?)

Any number may play.

Needed: A large ball.

The players form a circle. One player begins by bouncing the ball as he counts:

Uno, dos, tres, cuatro, (etc.)	One, two, three, four, (etc.)

When he makes a mistake or can count no further, another takes his place with the ball. Or the teacher may set a limit on the number of times each player may bounce the ball, after which he must pass it to another player, who repeats the same count.

PODEMOS CONTAR

(We can count)

Students can practice numbers as well as learn the Spanish names of their classmates in this game, which can be played by any number.

Needed: A large ball.

Children, who have all previously chosen Spanish names, stand in a circle. One player bounces the ball, counting to any number he chooses, once for each bounce. Other players count with him. Sometime during the count, he calls one of the other players, "María," for example, and tosses the ball to her. The child who catches the ball must say:

Me llamo María.   My name is Mary.

Then she bounces the ball and continues counting, accompanied by the others. In order that every child may have a turn, each player may be limited to ten bounces, after which he must throw the ball to someone.

BUSCA EL ANILLO

(Look for the ring)

As many as 40 may play.

Needed: A length of string or cord 12 to 18 inches long for each player and a metal or plastic ring.

Each player is given a piece of string which each must tie to that of her neighbor to make a continuous circle. Before the final knot is tied, the ring is slipped on the cord. The players form a circle holding the cord in their hands in front of them. A player stands in the middle of the circle. At a signal, the ring is passed rapidly along the cord at the same time that all the players say:

Busca el anillo	Look for the ring
pasando de mano	Passing from hand
en mano.	to hand.
Adivina quién lo tiene.	Guess who has it.

When these words have been spoken, all hands stop moving and the player in the center tries to guess who has the ring. If she guesses incorrectly, the chanting and passing are repeated and she tries again to guess. When she guesses correctly, she exchanges places with the one who held the ring.

Adapted from *Libro de Juegos*, page 4. Permission to reprint granted by the World Bureau Office of World Association of Girl Guides and Girl Scouts, New York.

HACIENDO AMISTADES
(Making friends)

Any number may play.

A circle is formed with one player in the center. Two minutes are allowed for each player to learn the first and last name of his neighbor to the left and to the right. The player in the center then turns about and with his arm extended says:

Izquierda	Left
o	or
Derecha	Right

As he does this he points to someone in the circle. The player indicated must give the name of his neighbor to the left or to the right, as indicated by the Leader, before the Leader in the center has counted to *diez* (ten). If the player confuses *izquierda* with *derecha,* or if he fails to give the name of his neighbor in the time allowed, he goes to the center of the circle and changes places with the person there.

Adapted from *Libro de Juegos,* page 7. Permission to reprint granted by the World Bureau Office of World Association of Girl Guides and Girl Scouts, New York City.

EL FERROCARRIL

(The railroad)

This game should have over 15 players to be played effectively.

Needed: A whistle for the Leader or teacher.

One of the players is designated *la locomotora* (the locomotive) and the other players form a circle. A cross marked on the ground or floor with chalk represents a station before each player except one. *La locomotora* runs around the outside of the circle and touches the other players in turn. As soon as each one is tagged, he must join the "train" behind the *locomotora*. As the train grows longer, the Leader, in the center of the circle will call out such expressions as:

¡Tren expreso!	Express train!
¡Hacia atrás!	Back up!
Despacio.	Slow.
Túnel.	Tunnel.

and any other directions which may be appropriate.

With each command, the train of players must act accordingly. When the Leader blows the whistle, the train pauses and everyone except the *locomotora* must scramble to reach a station. The one without a station is out of the game. One of the crosses is now erased, and the game continues, always with one more player than there are stations. The last child who remains with a station is declared the winner.

Adapted from *Libro de Juegos*, page 27. Permission to reprint granted by the World Bureau Office of the World Association of Girl Guides and Girl Scouts, New York City.

PAN Y QUESO
(Bread and cheese)

A traditional game of Mexico, this is somewhat like our "Pussy Wants a Corner." Any number may play.

A group forms a large circle or square. One of the players is chosen to be the *comprador* (buyer). He approaches one of those in the circle and asks:

¿En dónde se venden pan y queso?	Where do they sell bread and cheese?

The player approached, pointing to another, replies:

Ahí.	Over there.

The *comprador* walks over to the other player designated, and asks:

¿En dónde se venden pan y queso?

As he is doing this, the first player who answered tries to exchange places as quickly as possible with the player directly opposite him. The *comprador* tries to reach one of the empty places first. If he does, the one left without a place becomes the *comprador* and the game continues.

¿DONDE ESTA EL CONEJO?
(Where is the rabbit?)

About 20 may play.

Children kneel in a circle and each places his hand on the shoulder of the player next to him. One is selected to be *el conejo* (the rabbit) and is given a spot to be his home. The *conejo* runs around outside the ring, saying:

Soy el conejo.	I am the rabbit.

He runs around the circle several times, repeating this. Then he touches one of the kneeling children. The child says:

¿Dónde está el conejo?	Where is the rabbit?

The *conejo* answers:

Aquí estoy.	Here I am.

The player who has been touched stands up and begins to chase the rabbit. If the child cannot remember the words, *¿Dónde está el conejo?*, the *conejo* will go to another player in the circle, who repeats the question if he can. If the words are repeated correctly, the *conejo* starts running with the player in pursuit. If the *conejo* reaches his home without being tagged, he is safe, and the same action is repeated. If the *conejo* is caught, he changes places with the player and the game continues in the same way.

LAS CALABACITAS SE QUEMAN

(The squashes are burning)

This game is often played in Mexico by girls but any uneven number of pupils may play.

The girls take hands and form a circle. They walk around as they chant:

Las calabacitas se queman,	The squashes are burning,
se queman, se queman,	are burning, are burning,
y el que no se abraza	and the one who does not embrace
se queda, se queda.	is left, is left.

When the chant is finished, they stop circling and rush to find a partner and embrace her. One player is always left without a partner. The chant may be repeated as many times as desired.

LA RATA Y EL GATO

(The rat and the cat)

Ten or more players.

One of the players, *la rata* (rat), stands while the others form a circle about him. *El gato* (cat), is outside the circle. The *gato* taps one of those in the circle and the dialogue is as follows:

Gato:
Quisiera hablar con la rata.   I'd like to speak to the rat.
Player:
Ahora no.   Not now.
Gato:
¿Cuándo?   When?
Player:
A las doce.   At twelve o'clock.

As soon as the time has been mentioned, those in the circle start moving around rhythmically and chanting: "*la una, tic, toc; las dos, tic, toc; las tres, tic, toc . . .*" and so on until they reach *las doce* (twelve). They stop and the *gato* again steps to the circle and says:

Quisiera hablar con la rata.
Player:
   ¿Qué hora es?   What time is it?
Gato:
   Son las doce.   It's twelve o'clock.
Player:
   Está bien. Pase usted.   All right. Come in.

Those in the circle lift their arms, permitting the *gato* to enter. He chases the *rata* out of the circle. If the *rata* can circle the outside of the ring three times without being caught, he is safe and the game continues as before, with another *gato* and *rata* if desired.

Another version of the same game, with simpler dialogue.

Players join hands and form a circle, with the rat in the center and the cat outside. The circle moves to the left. The *gato* calls out to the *rata:*

   Soy el gato.   I'm the cat.
Rata:
   Soy la rata.   I'm the rat.
Gato:
   A que te agarro.   Bet I can catch you.
Rata:
   Si puedes.   Catch if you can.

At this the players in the circle raise their arms and the *rata* runs out of the circle to be pursued by the *gato*. After he has once run out of the circle, the *rata* may escape into the center through one of the "holes" formed by the upraised arms, provided he runs completely around the outside of the ring at least once. If the *rata* escapes into his hole, he is safe, and another *rata* may be chosen to take his place, as well as another *gato*, if desired. For more competition, the group may choose to have the boys take turns being the *gato* and the girls the *rata*, with points scored for each side as the game continues.

In some Spanish-speaking countries, the following dialogue is used in the game:

Gato:
   Ratón, ¿qué haces en mi huerto? — Rat, what are you doing in my vineyard?

Ratón:
   Como uvas. — I'm eating grapes.

Gato:
   Dame. — Give me some.

Ratón:
   Aquí tienes. — Here they are.

Gato:
   Dame algunas más. — Give me some more.

Ratón:
   No. — No.

Gato:
   A que te agarro. — I'll catch you.

Ratón:
   Si puedes. — Catch if you can.

EL HUESO

(The bone)

Up to 20 children may play.

Needed: A cardboard cut-out object resembling a bone may be made, if desired, or an object such as an eraser may be used. A chair is needed for each player, and a blindfold.

One player is chosen to be *el perro* (the dog). He sits blindfolded, supposedly sleeping. All other players sit in a circle around the *perro's* chair. At a signal from the Leader, a player in the circle stealthily attempts to get the *hueso* which has been placed under the *perro's* chair. If the *perro* hears the player, he stands up, and the player caught in the act must become the *perro.* If the child gets the *hueso* without awakening the *perro,* he hides it somewhere on his person, perhaps by sitting on it. When a player has done this, all those in the circle say:

¡Perro! ¡Perro! ¡Despiértate! Dog, dog, wake up!

The dog stands up, removes the blindfold, and goes around the circle, asking:

¿Quién tiene mi hueso? Who has my bone?

Turning to a player, he then asks:

Angelita, ¿tienes tú Angelita, do you have my bone?
mi hueso?

Player:
No, no tengo tu hueso. No, I don't have your bone.

The *perro* is allowed to ask three players the question. If he fails to find the bone on the third try, he must return to the center. If he finds the *hueso,* the one who hid it must take his place as the *perro.*

¿HAY CARTAS PARA MI?

(Are there letters for me?)

10 to 20 players.

Needed: A list of cities. Various pieces of mail in a bag. Chair for each player except one.

One player is assigned to be the *cartero* (mailman) and each of the other players is given the name of a city by the Leader. Then the players place chairs in a circle and sit down, except for the *cartero*, who remains in the center. Beside him on the floor is a bag that represents a mailbag. The *cartero* reaches into this bag and brings out a piece of mail, for example, a newspaper.

Cartero:

Tengo un periódico que va de La Paz a Buenos Aires.	I have a newspaper that is going from La Paz to Buenos Aires.

The two players who were assigned the names of these two cities jump up and try to exchange places. The *cartero*, however, dashes over in an attempt to sit on one of the chairs before one of the others. The one who is unsuccessful in sitting down is the next *cartero*. He goes to the center, reaches into the mailbag and brings out another piece of mail which he assigns to two cities in the same manner as before. The procedure is repeated with each exchange.

JUEGO DE PRENDAS

(Forfeits game)

Any number may play.

Needed: Several small articles for each child, such as a coin, a hairbow, an old key, a pencil—any trifle that a player is willing to give up and that might not be returned to him. A record player and a few recordings of Spanish songs. A plastic bowl.

The Leader explains that a circle will be formed. A Spanish song familiar to the group will be played while an empty plastic bowl is passed around by the players in the circle. When the music stops, the person who holds the bowl must show the others what his forfeit is and name it in Spanish. The music is resumed and the bowl again passed around the circle. When the music stops, the player holding the bowl must likewise pay a forfeit. This is repeated a few times. At the end of the song, the player with the bowl holds up the forfeits for the group to see. He keeps as many as he can correctly name in Spanish. The group corrects him in chorus and the unnamed forfeits remain in the bowl to be passed around the circle as before.

Another song is played and the bowl goes around a few more times, with more interruptions. The final player is permitted to keep the forfeits if he names them correctly.

In some versions, a player who has already forfeited something is allowed to name one of the objects in the bowl on his second turn and, if the name is correct, he may take the object out.

¿QUE HAY EN LA CAJA?

(What's in the box?)

Any number can play.

Needed: A group of small objects whose names are known to the students. These are selected and shown to the class before the game begins, and are then put out of sight. A box is needed, large enough to hold any one of the objects.

The player chosen as Leader selects an object and hides it in the box. The other players sit in a circle and try to guess what is in the box.

Leader:
 ¿Qué hay en la caja?   What's in the box?
Player 1:
 ¿Es una muñeca?   Is it a doll?
Leader:
 No es muñeca.   It isn't a doll.
 ¿Qué hay en la caja?
 (to another)
Player 2:
 ¿Es una pelota?   Is it a ball?
Leader:
 Sí, es pelota.   Yes, it's a ball.

The Leader asks each player in turn, until someone guesses correctly what is in the box. That player then becomes the Leader and chooses an object to hide in the box and the game continues.

¿SE VA A CAER?
(Is it going to fall?)

Any number of players.

Needed: A light basket.

One player places the basket on his head. The others form a circle around him.

Leader:

¿Se va a caer?	Is it going to fall?

Player:

No sé.	I don't know.

The other players start walking around him in a circle. The Leader orders the player with the basket:

¡A la derecha!	To the right!
o	
¡A la izquierda!	To the left!

The player turns his head as instructed, as the other players begin to count to twenty (or thirty, if desired). If the basket falls before the count is completed, all the players say:

Se cayó la canasta.	The basket fell.

In that case, the Leader chooses another to stand in the center with the basket on his head. If the basket remains balanced for the full count, the player in the center may choose the player to take his place.

LA REINA SE ESTA BAÑANDO

(The queen is taking a bath)

Nine children play this traditional game of Venezuela.

Needed: 8 chairs.

A circle is formed by eight children seated on chairs. One girl, *la reina* (the queen), remains standing. To each of the children seated she gives a name corresponding to one of the articles that the *reina* will need when she takes a bath, for example: *jabón* (soap); *champú* (shampoo); *peine* (comb); *cepillo para la cabeza* (hairbrush); *toalla* (towel); *perfume*, etc. The *reina* walks around the circle of children and says, at first speaking very slowly:

La reina se va a bañar	The Queen is going to
y necesita . . .	take a bath and she needs . . .

Now speaking very rapidly:

. . . ¡el jabón!	. . . soap!

The child who has the name of *jabón* gets up and follows the *reina* as she continues to walk around the circle. Again she says slowly:

La reina se va a bañar y necesita . . .

Quickly:

. . . ¡la toalla!	. . . the towel!

The game continues in this manner until all the children have left their seats and are following her around the circle of chairs. Then the *reina* says:

Se está bañando la reina,	The Queen is taking a bath . . .
se está bañando la reina.	

After repeating this two or three times, she sits down on one of the chairs and says:

Se sentó la reina.	The Queen sat down.

All the children scramble to find a chair. One will be left out and she will become the next *reina*.

EL ESPEJO

(The mirror)

Up to 30 may play.

Needed: A mirror labeled *El espejo* is optional.

The Leader starts the game by choosing the first player. The others form a circle around him.

Player 1 to Leader:
¿Tiene usted un buen espejo?	Have you a good mirror?

Leader, indicating circle:
Escoja usted.	Choose.

Player 1:
Gracias.	Thank you.

He chooses one in the circle who will be his *espejo,* that is, imitate exactly the words Player 1 may speak, any song he may sing or gestures he may make. Player 1 may sing a simple song in Spanish or count, or name the days of the week, or recite a short poem. When the mirror has faithfully imitated Player 1, the latter says to the Leader:

Escojo este espejo.	I choose this mirror.

Leader:
Muy bien.	All right.

The *espejo* then becomes Player 2 and the game continues in the same manner.

UN REFRAN

El mejor espejo es un buen amigo.

(The best mirror is a good friend.)

¿QUE FALTA EN LA TORTA?

(What is missing in the cake?)

10 or 11 players.

Needed: A large spoon and a large bowl. A sign for each player except for the *cocinero,* showing a picture of a particular ingredient for a cake. Under the picture is the name in Spanish, for example, a picture of two eggs and the words *dos huevos.*

A circle is formed. In the center the *cocinero* (cook), blindfolded, pretends to be vigorously stirring with a large spoon the cake batter in the bowl. The players in the circle dance around him and say:

Algo falta en la torta.   Something is missing in
                                the cake.

The blindfolded *cocinero* points to someone in the circle and asks:

¿Qué falta en la torta?   What is missing in the cake?

The player indicated answers as he shows his picture:

Falta la leche en la torta.   The cake lacks milk.

He leaves the circle to stand beside the *cocinero* and join him in saying:

¿Qué falta en la torta?

The blindfolded *cocinero* again indicates someone in the circle and the player shows his picture and replies. The game continues until all ingredients have been added to the cake.

Vocabulary for ¿QUE FALTA EN LA TORTA?

la leche	milk
la harina	flour
la levadura	baking powder
la mantequilla	butter
la sal	salt
los huevos	eggs
las almendras	almonds
el chocolate	chocolate
el azúcar	sugar
la vainilla	vanilla

The teacher may select other appropriate ingredients.

EL CUMPLEAÑOS

(The birthday)

About ten may play.

Needed: Pictures of various gifts with the Spanish name under each picture, if desired.

The players form a circle and sing to the tune of "Happy Birthday to You":

Felicidades a ti,		*Cumpleaños feliz,*
felicidades a ti,	or	*cumpleaños feliz,*
felicidades a ti,		*cumpleaños feliz,*
felicidades a ti.		*cumpleaños feliz.*

The first player says:

El día de mi cumpleaños, recibí unos dulces.

On my birthday I received some candy.

Player 2:

El día de mi cumpleaños, recibí unos dulces y un disco.

. . . I received some candy and a record.

Player 3:

El día de mi cumpleaños, recibí unos dulces, un disco y un libro.

. . . I received some candy, a record, and a book.

The game continues around the circle. Each player must add one more item to the gift list, repeating all those previously named if he can. Each gift that the player lists counts a point for him and the winner is the one with the most points when the game ends.

EL LOBO SE VISTE

(The wolf dresses himself)

This is a traditional tag game of Spanish-speaking countries which any number may play.

Needed: A hat, coat, shirt, gloves, and other articles of man's clothing.

One player is chosen to be the *lobo* (wolf). He stands beside a few articles of clothing, and the other players form a circle around him. They call to him:

Señor Lobo, señor Lobo.	Mr. Wolf, Mr. Wolf,
¿Listo?	are you ready?
Lobo:	
No estoy listo. Tengo	I'm not ready. I have
que ponerme la camisa.	to put on my shirt.

The *lobo* puts the shirt on over his own.

Señor Lobo, señor Lobo.	
¿Listo?	
Lobo:	
No estoy listo. Tengo	. . . I have to put on my hat.
que ponerme el sombrero.	

He puts on the hat. He may put on all the articles of clothing or, at any time, he may say if he wishes:

Listo, sí. Ahí voy.	I'm ready and here I come.
¡Ahora les agarro!	Now I'll get you!

The players rush to a designated safety zone with the *lobo* in pursuit. He tries to tag a player before he reaches the safety zone. The tagged player becomes the *lobo* as the game continues.

EN EL MAR, EN LA PLAYA

(In the sea, on the beach)

An active outdoor game which as many as 40 can play.

A line is drawn, dividing the playing area into two parts, *el mar* (the sea) and *la playa* (the beach), and the players stand on the line. If the Leader calls out, *"¡El mar!"*, all the players must jump to the side so designated. If the Leader calls out, *"¡La playa!"*, all the players jump to the other side. The Leader may call out the commands very quickly in an effort to have the players jump in the wrong direction or at the wrong time. Anyone jumping in the wrong direction or failing to jump at the command must leave the game. The last one remaining is the winner.

SOL Y SOMBRA

(Sun and shade)

Any number may play this traditional game of Central America.

Two parallel lines are drawn enclosing a neutral zone with a goal at each end. Players are divided into two groups, *sol* (sun) and *sombra* (shade), and each group is assigned to a goal. The Leader tosses a coin. If it comes up "heads," he calls *"¡Sol!"*, and if "tails," *"¡Sombra!"* Whichever the Leader calls, the players on that side must try to tag those on the other side before they can get to their safety goal. When a player is tagged, he must go to the other side. As players tag, they call out *"¡Sol!"* or *"¡Sombra!"*. The side with the most players at the end of the game is the winner.

MI CORDERO

(My lamb)

20 is a good number of players for this game, but any number may play.

One person is chosen to be the *pastor* (shepherd) and is blindfolded. The other players form a line facing him. The blindfolded *pastor*, walking along the line, may stop when he wishes, choose a player facing him, and ask him:

¿Dónde está mi cordero?	Where is my lamb?
He perdido mi cordero.	I have lost my lamb.

The one standing opposite him disguises his voice and replies:

Yo soy su cordero.	I'm your lamb.
Pastor:	
¿Eres Paco?	Are you Paco?

The *pastor* has two chances to guess the identity of the *cordero*. If he does not guess correctly, he tries someone else. When he guesses correctly, he and the *cordero* change places.

Some play the game with the *pastor* removing the blindfold when he has guessed correctly and chasing the *cordero*. He must tag the *cordero* before he can change places with him.

¿QUIEN TIENE MIEDO DEL TIGRE?

(Who's afraid of the tiger?)

Ten or more may play this game.

There are two goal lines with the players at one of them. The *tigre* (tiger) is waiting on the sidelines. The *tigre* calls out to the players:

¿Quién tiene miedo del tigre?	Who's afraid of the tiger?

Player 1:

Yo no.	Not I.

Player 2:

Yo no tengo miedo.	I'm not afraid.

Player 3:

Nadie tiene miedo.	No one is afraid.

No one may start running for the opposite goal until the above dialogue is completed. Once it is, the players rush for the other goal with the *tigre* in pursuit. While running, all players must shout such words as:

¡Ahí viene el tigre!	Here comes the tiger!
Tengo miedo.	I'm afraid.
¡Yo también tengo miedo!	I'm afraid, too!
¡Socorro!	Help!

Any player touched by the *tigre* is considered caught and must become a tiger helper until all players are helping the *tigre*. The last player caught is the new *tigre*.

¿QUIEN ES?

(Who is it?)

A blindfold game that any number may play.

One of the players, Player 1, is blindfolded and another player, Player 2, shakes hands with him and says:

Buenos días.	Good morning.
(Buenas tardes.)	(or Good afternoon.)

Player 1:

Buenos días. ¿Quién es?	Good morning. Who is it?

Player 2:
  Soy amigo (amiga).   I'm a friend.

Player 1:
  ¿Es Leonardo?   Is it Leonardo?

If the player has guessed correctly, the others in the group answer:

  Sí, es Leonardo.   Yes, it's Leonardo.

If the player has guessed incorrectly, the others in the group answer:

  No, no es Leonardo.   No, it isn't Leonardo.

Each blindfolded player has three chances to guess the identity of the player who has shaken his hand. If he guesses on the first try, he gains three points, two points on the second try, one point on the third, and no points if he fails to guess at all. Students may be divided into two teams for more excitement. In that case, one player from each team is blindfolded alternately and the points are scored for the team according to the pattern described.

LA GALLINITA CIEGA
(The little blind hen)

Up to 40 may play.

One player, blindfolded, takes the part of the *gallinita ciega* (little blind hen), and imitates her scratching for food. The other players form a circle about her, saying:

  Gallinita ciega, ¿qué andas   Little blind hen,
    buscando?   what are you looking for?

Gallinita:
  Unos granitos.   A few grains.

Players:
   ¿Para quién?   For whom?

Gallinita:
   Para mis pollitos.   For my little chicks.

Players:
   ¿Y nos darás uno?   And will you give us one?

Gallinita:
   No.

Players:
   Pues, ¡piérdelos!   Then, lose them!

At this, the *gallinita* chases the players. Whoever is caught becomes the next *gallinita* and the game continues.

❈   ❈   ❈   ❈   ❈

The following version of the game is played in some Spanish-speaking countries.

One player is blindfolded and the others ask her:

Gallinita ciega, ¿qué se te   Little blind hen, what
   ha perdido?   have you lost?

Gallinita:
   Una aguja y un dedal.   A needle and a thimble.

Players:
   Pues, da tres vueltas y   Well, turn around three times
   los hallarás.   and you'll find them.

One of the players turns the *gallinita* around three times and then once in reverse. The *gallinita* chases the players. Whoever is caught becomes the *gallinita* and the game continues as before.

VOY A COMPRAR UN POLLO

(I'm going to buy a chicken)

In this game there are the *vendedor* (seller), the *comprador* (buyer), and five or six children who are the *pollos* (chickens).

The *pollos* pretend they are in a market. They stoop down with their hands clasped under their knees. The *comprador* comes up to the *vendedor* and says:

¿Qué tal los pollos?	How are the chickens?
¿Tiernos?	Tender?

Vendedor:

Sí, señor (señora),	Yes, sir (madam),
muy tiernos.	very tender.

The *comprador* gets behind the row of *pollos* and puts his hand on each *pollo*'s head in turn, saying:

Este pollo no es tierno.	This chicken isn't tender.

He tries another:

Este pollo no es tierno.	This chicken isn't tender.
Es viejo.	It's old.

or

Este pollo no es tierno.	. . .
Es gordo.	It's fat.

He finally selects one and says:

Este pollo es tierno.	This chicken is tender.
Me lo llevo.	I'll take it.

At this, the *pollo* must jump up and say:

¿Yo? No, señor. Adiós.	Me? No, sir. Goodbye.

The *pollo* runs away, the *comprador* in pursuit. If the *comprador* catches the *pollo*, the latter becomes the *comprador* and the game continues.

LA VIEJA INES

(Old Ines)

Eight children may play this game, to practice the names of colors.

Two players are chosen as *la vieja Inés*, and the *madre* (mother). The others are the *madre*'s children and each one takes the name of a color. Each takes his place behind the *madre*. A large circle is marked on the ground some distance away. *La vieja Inés* faces the *madre*, pretends to knock on a door, and says:

Tan, tan.	Knock, knock.
Madre:	
¿Quién es?	Who is it?
Inés:	
La vieja Inés.	Old Ines.
Madre:	
¿Qué quieres?	What do you want?
Inés:	
Quiero colores.	I want colors.
Madre:	
¿Qué color quieres?	What color do you want?
Inés:	
Quiero rojo (or any other color she wishes)	I want red.

The player who is *rojo* runs away, followed by *la vieja Inés*. He tries to reach the home base circle before he is caught. If he does so, he is allowed to return to his place behind the *madre*. The game continues until all the colors have been both chosen and caught by *la vieja Inés*. The last one to be caught becomes the *madre* and the game goes on with a new *Inés*.

LAS ESCONDIDAS
(The hiders)

The game may be played by a small group or as many as 30. It is "Hide and Seek" with Spanish words.

A spy is chosen. He takes his place at a tree or something that serves as a goal. The other players scatter and hide. The spy closes his eyes, puts his arm across his eyes, and counts:

Uno, dos, tres, cuatro, etc.   One, two, three, four.
—and on to 20.

Then the spy turns, takes his arm away from his eyes, and looks around as he says:

Uno, dos, tres. ¡Cuidado!   One, two, three. Watch out!
¡Ahí voy!   Here I come!

He starts out to seek the players who are hiding. When he discovers one, the spy runs back to the goal. The player hiding comes out and races the spy to the goal. If the spy reaches the goal first, he touches it and says:

Uno, dos, tres . . . Juan.   One, two, three . . . John.

If the player reaches the goal before the spy, he touches it and calls out:

Me salvé.   I am safe.

The first player who is caught by the spy changes places with him for the next game.

✿ ✿ ✿ ✿ ✿

In another version of the game, as played in various Spanish-speaking countries, the spy counts to 40 while the others hide. Then he shouts:

¡Cuareeeeenta matas!   Forty kills!
                        (Coming, ready or not!)

and goes to look for the other players. The game continues in the manner described.

EL LOBO
(The wolf)

Any number may play.

Needed: If desired, there may be a sign with a picture of a wolf and the words "*El lobo.*" The mother may also have a sign pinned to her dress, "*La madre.*"

One of the players introduces the others: "*El lobo, la madre y los niños* (children)."

The *lobo* pretends to hide behind a bush or tree, or behind the sign. The players go to the *madre* in their "house," a circle marked on the ground. One of the *niños* says to the *madre:*

Por favor, mamá, déjanos jugar.	Please, Mama, let us play.

Niño 2:

Sí, mamá, déjanos, por favor.	Yes, Mama, let us, please.

Madre:

Bueno . . . pero, cuidado con el lobo.	All right . . . but watch out for the wolf.

The *niños* run out to play and call to the *lobo:*

¡Señor Lobo! ¡Ven! ¡Ven acá, señor Lobo!	Mr. Wolf, come. Come here, Mr. Wolf!

The *lobo* comes out from his hiding place and chases the *niños.* The *niños* call out, saying such things as:

¡Socorro! ¡Socorro!	Help, help!
¡El lobo! ¡Mamá! ¡Socorro!	The wolf! Mama! Help!

Those who are caught by the *lobo* become his helpers, and the game continues as before until all the *niños* have been caught.

MEDIANOCHE
(Midnight)

Ten or more may play.

Needed: Signs may be used if desired, one for *el zorro* (the fox) and one for *las ovejas* (the sheep). At one side where the fox will stand, there may be a picture of a fox. At the opposite side there may be a sign with a picture of sheep.

The announcer introduces *el zorro*. The *zorro* comes out from his side and walks about. The *ovejas* rush out from their place, shouting:

¡Ahí viene el zorro!   Here comes the fox!

They go as close to him as they dare and say:

Señor Zorro, ¿qué hora es?   Mr. Fox, what time is it?

The *zorro* will name any hour he wishes, such as:

Son las cinco.   It's five o'clock.

The *ovejas* repeat their question and the *zorro* may reply with any hour. But when the *zorro* says:

¡Las doce! ¡Medianoche!   Twelve! Midnight!
the *ovejas* run as fast as they can with the *zorro* after them, all shouting:

¡No! ¡No! ¡Ahí viene!   No, no! Here he comes!
¡Socorro!   Help!
¡No, señor Zorro!   No, Mr. Fox!

When one of the *ovejas* has been caught, he becomes the *zorro*, and the game is played again.

EL CARTERO

(The mailman)

A game for jumping rope played by girls in Venezuela.

Two girls begin the game by each taking the opposite end of a jump rope. The others form a group. One takes the part of the *cartero*, and the following dialogue takes place between her and the two girls holding the jump rope:

¡Tan, tan!	Knock, knock.

Las niñas con la cuerda
  en la mano:
  ¿Quién es?
	Who is it?

Cartero: *El cartero.*	
Niñas: *¿Qué desea?*	What do you want?
Cartero: *Una carta.*	A letter.
Niñas: *¿Para quién?*	For whom?

At this point the *cartero* names one of the other girls, for example:

Para Carmen.

Niñas: *¿De cuántas líneas?*	How many lines?
Cartero: *De diez (cien, etc.)*	Ten (a hundred, etc.)

Then the *cartero* has to jump rope as many times as the number of lines mentioned. Usually she gives a large number in order to demonstrate her skill. If she tires or stumbles, she loses and must leave the game and pay a forfeit. The girl to whom the letter was addressed is the next *cartero*.

EL JARDINERO Y LOS LADRONES
(The gardener and the thieves)

This game needs a fairly large number of players.

One group of children in a circle represents the *jardín* (garden). Inside the *jardín* are several *ladrones* (thieves). They go through the motions of reaching for apples on a tree and of eating the fruit. One player who has been chosen as the *jardinero* (gardener) enters the *jardín* and asks:

¿Qué hacen aquí?	What are you doing here?
Ladrón 1:	
Pues, comiendo manzanas, señor.	Why, eating apples, sir.
Jardinero:	
¿Quién les dio permiso?	Who gave you permission?
Ladrón 2:	
Pues, nadie, señor.	Why, no one, sir.
Jardinero:	
¡Fuera de aquí! ¡Fuera de aquí! ¡Váyanse!	Out of here! Get out!

The *jardinero* chases the *ladrones* and catches those that he can. Once the *ladrones* are outside the *jardín*, they are safe.

A LA VIBORA

(To the serpent)

Children of El Salvador play this game with about 30 players. There are other versions in most Spanish-speaking countries. It is similar to the English "London Bridge."

Two of the tallest boys or girls are chosen from among the players and are called *San Pablo* (St. Paul) and *San Pedro* (St. Peter). They form an arch with their hands held high and keep this position throughout the game. The other players form a line, each one placing his hands on the shoulders of the one preceding him, as they walk toward the arch, saying:

A la víbora, a la víbora de la mar,	To the serpent, to the serpent of the sea,
por aquí quieren pasar,	Through here they want to go.
y los de atrás se quedarán.	And those in back will remain
¡Tras! ¡Tras! ¡Tras!	Behind! Behind! Behind!

When nearly all the children have passed through the arch, *San Pedro* and *San Pablo* lower their arms and "catch" one of the last. Either *San Pedro* or *San Pablo* asks the captured one:

¿Con quién quieres ir? ¿Con San Pedro o con San Pablo?	With whom do you want to go? With St. Peter or St. Paul?

The player chooses the one he wishes and starts the beginning of a line in back of either "saint." The game continues until no one is left in the original line. Sometimes, the two groups have a tug of war to determine which saint is the stronger.

LA FRUTA

(The fruit)

A Peruvian game played by any number of girls and boys.

The players sit on the ground and the Leader whispers the name of a fruit to each player and remembers one for himself. No one is supposed to know the name of each other's fruit. Two players act as *el Angel* and *el Diablo* (Devil). The *Angel* approaches a player and says:

Tin, tan.	Knock, knock.
Player:	
¿Quién?	Who is it?
Angel:	
El ángel con la taza de oro.	The angel with the gold cup.
Player:	
¿Qué quiere?	What do you want?
Angel:	
Quiero fruta.	I want fruit.
Player:	
¿Qué clase de fruta?	What kind of fruit?

The *Angel* then guesses the name of a fruit. If he guesses correctly, the player becomes a member of his team and steps to one side. If the *Angel* does not guess right, he waits until the *Diablo* has had a turn. *Angel* and *Diablo* alternate until all the players are on one team or the other. When the *Diablo* knocks, he says:

El diablo con los 40,000 cuernos.	The devil with the 40,000 horns.

The players end with a tug of war to decide the winning team.

Vocabulary for the game:

mangos	mangos
plátanos	bananas
piñas	pineapples
manzanas	apples
peras	pears
naranjas	oranges
toronjas	grapefruit
ciruelas	plums
cerezas	cherries
fresas	strawberries
papayas	papayas

and any others desired.

Adapted from *Hi Neighbor*, Book 6, United States Committee for UNICEF, Hastings House Publishers, New York, pages 46-7. Permission to reprint granted by the publishers.

ARRANCA CEBOLLAS

(Pull out onions)

Señorita Alida Escobar of San Salvador, El Salvador, says this game is one of the favorites of children of her country, with a good-sized number of players.

From the players are chosen *el vendedor* (seller) and *el comprador* (buyer). In the game, the *comprador* tries to pull away the *cebollas* (onions) from the *vendedor*. The *vendedor* must hold on with both arms to a tree or pole. The other players are the *cebollas*, and one clasps his arms around the waist of the *vendedor*. Each player clasps his arms around the waist of the player in front of him so that a string of *cebollas* is formed. The *comprador* now approaches the *vendedor* and asks:

¿Quieres vender?	Do you want to sell?

Vendedor:

No las vendo.	I'm not selling them.

Comprador:
 ¿Por qué?   Why?

Vendedor:
 Porque no se dejan Because they can't be pulled
  arrancar.   out. They are very tough.
 Están muy duras.

Comprador:
 ¡A que las arranco! Bet I can pull them out!

Vendedor:
 A que no.   Bet you can't.

Comprador:
 A que sí.   Bet I can.

They repeat this for several rounds with the *comprador* saying: "*A que sí*" and the *vendedor* saying: "*A que no.*" Then the *comprador* tries to pull someone from the tail of the string of *cebollas*, as the children hold on firmly. If the *comprador* succeeds in pulling away a *cebolla*, the player becomes the property of the *comprador*. The *comprador* tugs until he succeeds in getting as many away from the string of *cebollas* as possible. Of course, the *vendedor*, with his arms gripping the tree, is the most difficult one to pull away.

EL SOMBRERO VIEJO
(The old hat)

This is a game for ten players on each of two sides.

Needed: An old hat. A referee.

Each player is given a number and they place themselves in the following positions:

Side one: 1   2   3   4   5   6   7   8   9   10

El sombrero (the hat)

Side two: 10   9   8   7   6   5   4   3   2   1

The referee calls out: "*¡El sombrero!*" Then he calls out a number such as "*cinco*" (five). Players on each side having the number race for the *sombrero*, and the one who reaches it first snatches it up and shouts:

¡Lo tengo! ¡Tengo el   I have it! I have the hat!
sombrero!

If he cannot remember the phrase, he cannot pick up the *sombrero*. The onlookers say the phrase for him and the other side receives the point. Every time the player repeats the phrase correctly and picks up the hat, he makes a point for his side. The referee settles any dispute.

✿   ✿   ✿   ✿   ✿

Another version requires several objects to be placed in the center. When the referee calls out the name of one of the objects and a number, each player must attempt to snatch up only the object named. Thus, the players must know the Spanish name for each of the objects in the center before they can attempt to pick them up.

II Classroom Games

NOMBRES ESPAÑOLES

(Spanish names)

When Spanish names are familiar to a group of children, this game may be played by a whole class.

Needed: A blackboard.

On the board are written the headings *Niños* (Boys) and *Niñas* (Girls). The boys form one team and the girls the other. A child raises his hand and calls out a Spanish name, and the Leader at the blackboard writes down the name called out, under the appropriate heading. The team which has the greater number of Spanish names, at the end of a set time limit, is the winner.

Then the children repeat in chorus the names written on the board. Or the girls may listen to the boys repeat the names and say *"Muy bien"* (Very good). Then the boys will listen to the girls repeat the names and say *"Muy bien."*

The lists of names might look like this:

Niños	*Niñas*
Francisco	*María*
Pedro	*Rosa*
José	*Lupe*
Jorge, etc.	*Elena*, etc.

LOS TRES AMIGOS
(The three friends)

Each child may make his own drawings at his seat or three children at a time may be chosen to draw at the blackboard.

The first child draws a picture of the heads of three of his friends and under each one prints his or her Spanish name. The second child now draws a hat on each head. The hats may be funny, or whatever the child wishes. The third child writes under each picture:

El sombrero de Nelita	Nelita's hat
El sombrero de Paco	Paco's hat
El sombrero de Juan.	Juan's hat.

or whatever the names of the pictures may be.

ADIVINELO
(Guess it)

Any number may play this game.

Needed: A number of articles or pictures of articles, the Spanish names of which are known to the students.

One player is chosen to turn his back on the group. The Leader asks the group:

¿Listos?	Ready?

Players:

Sí, señorita, estamos listos.	Yes, senorita, we are ready.

The Leader shows the article selected to the group. The player with his back turned asks:

¿Es un libro?	Is it a book?

Players:

No, no es un libro.	No, it's not a book.

Player 1:

¿Es una flor?	Is it a flower?

The player has three chances to guess. If he cannot guess correctly, he turns around to face the group and all in chorus tell what it is. Then someone else takes a turn.

¿QUE ES?
(What is it?)

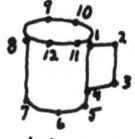

Any familiar object may be used for a dot picture on the blackboard.

One child connects the dots, counting the numbers aloud in Spanish. Another child names the article in Spanish when he finishes, or writes the name under the picture. Children may enjoy making their own dot pictures of objects whose Spanish names they know.

¿QUE COMPRA JOSE?
(What does José buy?)

On the blackboard is drawn a picture of a boy. Give him a Spanish name, like José. Opposite his picture children take turns drawing pictures of things they can name in Spanish that they want José to buy. With each picture, the class says, or writes:

José compra plátanos.	José buys bananas.
José compra dulces.	José buys candy.
José compra chicle.	José buys chewing gum.
etc.	

¿DONDE ESTA?

(Where is it?)

Up to 40 may play.

Needed: Any convenient object to be hidden.

One player is sent out of the room and the others decide upon a pencil, a key, etc. to be placed somewhere in the room. One of the players goes to the door and speaks to the person who has been sent out:

Pase usted.	Come in.

Player 1:
Gracias.	Thank you.

As Player 1 comes in, another player asks him:

¿Dónde está el lápiz?	Where is the pencil?
(la llave, etc.)	(the key, etc.)

Player 1:
No sé.	I don't know.

Player 3:
Búsquelo (la).	Look for it.

Player 1 begins to search for the object as the group counts in unison: "*Uno, dos, tres,* etc." They count as far as they wish to go. When Player 1 approaches the hidden article, their voices are raised; when Player 1 goes farther away, the words are spoken softly. When the object has been found, Player 1 holds it up before the class and says:

Aquí está. Aquí está	Here it is. Here's the pencil.
el lápiz.	

(Once a red pencil was hidden in a girl's pony tail and the player never did discover it.)

* * * * *

Another way to play the game:

While Player 1 is looking for the object, the group says in unison the days of the week, or the months of the year.

* * * * *

In English-speaking countries, we say in unison: "You're cold" or "You're hot." In some Spanish-speaking countries, the players say these words to the seeker:

Frío, frío, frío,	Cold cold, cold,
como las aguas del río.	like the waters of the river.

When the player approaches the hidden object the players say:

Calor, calor, calor, que se	Heat, heat, heat, that burns,
quema, que se quema . . .	burns . . .

LO VEO

(I see it)

Any number of players, divided into two teams.

Needed: A small object that is to be hidden. It may be a book, a red pencil, an eraser, or the like.

The Leader picks up the object to be hidden and announces:

Vamos a esconder este lápiz	Let's hide this pencil
(libro, borrador).	(book, eraser).

The first team leaves the room and the Leader hides the object in plain sight, yet in a way not easy to detect, such as on the windowsill or in the corner. The players outside return to the room and the Leader tells them:

Ya escondimos el lápiz.	Now we've hidden the pencil.

When a player sees the object, he says *"Lo veo"* and, instead of pointing it out, he sits down. One by one, the players discovering the "hidden" object will say *"Lo veo"* and sit down. The game continues until one or two players remain. The player who discovered the object first then goes to it, picks it up and says:

Aquí está. Aquí está el lápiz.	Here it is. Here is the pencil.

The object is hidden again and the other team tries to find it. The winning team is the one needing the shorter time for all players but one or two to locate the object.

EL CONDUCTOR DEL TREN

(The conductor of the train)

Any number may play.

Needed: Flash cards, each with a picture of a person or an object already familiar to students. Such as *el niño* (boy), *la niña* (girl), *el lápiz* (pencil), etc.

The players sit in a row of chairs. One player is chosen as *el conductor* (the conductor) and stands behind one of the players' chairs. The Leader shows a card with the picture and the player in the chair tries to say the word for it before the *conductor*, standing behind him, can do so. A score is kept. On the next race, the *conductor* moves to stand behind the chair of the next child and the game continues.

VOY A COMPRAR...

(I'm going to buy . . .)

Any number may play, in two teams.

Needed: A coin.

The first player on the first team shows a coin and says:

Tengo dinero.   I have money. I'm
Voy a comprar . . .   going to buy . . .

The player then pantomimes what he wants to buy, such as a horse, a boat, a ball, or something else. The first player on the second team, in turn, calls out the name of the object that is being pantomimed. Only words already familiar to players are used. If the second player cannot say the correct word in Spanish, another tries. If no one on his team can say the word for the object, the other team receives a point. If the second team succeeds in naming the object, it receives a point.

LAVO LA ROPA

(I wash clothes)

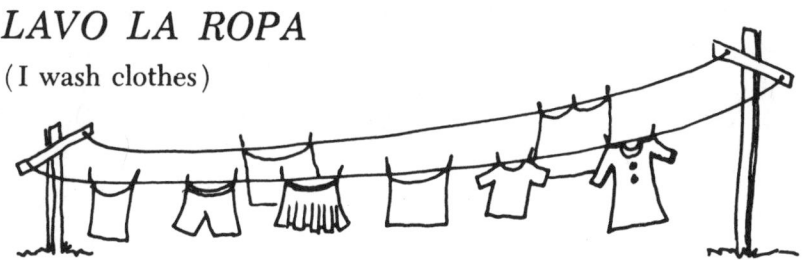

Up to 25 players may play this game in which the names of articles of clothing can be learned.

Needed: Dolls' clothing such as a dress, a skirt, a shirt; or articles of clothing may be cut from scraps of cloth or construction paper. A toy clothesline and clothespins, and a toy washtub, if desired.

Each child in the group takes a turn at picking up an article of clothing and pretending to wash it and hang it up. Indicating the article, the player says:

La falda. La falda amarilla.   The skirt, the yellow skirt.
Lavo la falda.   I wash the skirt.

The child hangs the skirt on the clothesline and another child takes her place, choosing another article of clothing and proceeding in the same manner. The game continues until everyone in the group has had a turn.

PELEA DE GALLOS

(Cockfight)

Two children at a time hold a mock cockfight and their knowledge of colors is also put to a test.

Needed: Pins and construction paper of different colors.

The two children face each other, with hands on their hips and elbows forward a little, as though they were wings. On each child's back is pinned a piece of colored construction paper. The children twist and turn, imitating a cockfight. They are not allowed to touch each other as they move around. Each one tries to see what color is pinned on the other's back, and, of course, each tries to keep the other from seeing what color is on his own back. When one of them succeeds in seeing the other's color, he calls out:

Verde (blanco, azul,
  amarillo, etc.)
	Green (White, blue, yellow,
	  etc.)

The onlookers cheer them on, shouting:

¡Olé! or *¡Anda!* or *¡Qué bueno!* or *¡Bravo!*	Hurray! Go to it! Good!

The game continues with two other players and other colors.

From *Beginning Lessons for Teaching Spanish to Small Children,* by Elizabeth L. Etnire, Division of Field Services, Central Michigan College, Mt. Pleasant, Michigan. Reprinted by permission of the author.

EL RELOJ GRANDE

(The big clock)

This game is for young children learning to tell time. Twelve children are the hours and the rest are spectators.

One child stands before the group with his arms held overhead and his palms together. Then he moves slowly from one side to another as he says:

Tique, toque, tique, toque.   Tick, tock, tick, tock.

Then he indicates some hour of his choice by pretending to be the clock striking:

Dindán.

The entire group then answers:

Son las dos.   It's two o'clock.

Another child pretends to be the clock in the same way, and the group must announce the hour he has "struck." The game ends when all the hours have been announced.

LA ORQUESTA

(The orchestra)

A small class can play this game to learn the Spanish names for musical instruments.

Needed: A variety of toy musical instruments, one for each child in the group.

One child is chosen to hold each of the musical instruments. The Leader points to one, for example, the one with the drum, saying:

Este toca el tambor.   This one beats the drum.

The other children repeat the word for the musical instrument:

El tambor.

The child beats the drum and the others imitate his action, saying:

¡Pon! ¡Pon! ¡Pon!

The Leader indicates another child in the same way, and the rest of the group repeat the word for his instrument and imitate him as he plays it.

SIMON DICE

(Simon says)

The class practices recognizing the names of the parts of the body as they play.

The players stand before the Leader, who says:

Simón dice: la cabeza.   Simon says: the head.

As the Leader says: "*Simón dice,*" he points to the part of the body he is naming. He may give the name of any part of the body he wishes as the game proceeds. But if he does not precede the name with "*Simón dice,*" the players are not supposed to imitate his action. If he does say "*Simón dice,*" the players must imitate him. Any player who fails to follow the Leader, or who points to the part of the body when "*Simón dice*" has not preceded it, is out of the game and must sit down. The game continues as the Leader names the parts of the body at will until only one player is left standing.

Some teachers prefer to have the students repeat the word that they are supposed to point to.

¿QUE DICEN LOS ANIMALES?

(What do the animals say?)

Any number may play.

Needed: A number of pictures of animals.

Children take turns showing a picture to the group. One child may show a picture of chickens and all the children must say in chorus:

Los pollitos dicen —pío, pío.   Chickens say peep, peep.

As other children show pictures, the group says in unison, according to the picture, such words as:

El gallo dice,	The cock says "Cocka doodle-
"Quiquirriquí."	do."
El gato dice, "Miau, miau."	The cat says "Meow, meow."
La vaca dice, "Mu, mu."	The cow says "Moo, moo."
El burro dice, "Jija, jija."	The burro says, "Hee-haw."
El perro dice, "Guau, guau."	The dog says, "Bow, wow."
La oveja dice, "Maa, maa."	The sheep says, "Baa, baa."

LOS ANIMALES GRANDES Y LOS ANIMALES PEQUEÑOS

(Large animals and small animals)

The game may be played by two teams.

Needed: Pictures of the following animals: lion, giraffe, dog, lamb, duck, elephant, mouse, cat, and any other animal desired.

Teams are selected. The Leader asks questions similar to those below of individual students on each team, in turn. Each correct answer scores a point for the team. If a player on one team fails to answer correctly, the other team gets a chance at the question.

¿Cuántos animales grandes hay?	How many large animals are there?
¿Cuántos animales pequeños hay?	How many small animals are there?
¿Cómo se llaman los animales grandes?	What are the names of the large animals?
¿Cómo se llaman los animales pequeños?	What are the names of the small animals?
¿Cuál de los animales es el más grande de todos?	Which of the animals is the largest of all?
¿Cuál de los animales vive en la selva?	Which of the animals lives in the jungle?
etc.	

¿DONDE ESTA?

(Where is it?)

Any number may play.

One player is sent out of the classroom. The rest decide on an object in the room. When the player returns, he must try to find out what the object is. He must do so by asking questions that can be answered by "yes" or "no." The other players take turns answering his questions. He may ask:

¿Es amarillo?	Is it yellow?
Player:	
Sí, es amarillo.	Yes, it's yellow.
Guesser:	
¿Es grande?	Is it large?
Another player:	
No, no es grande.	No, it isn't large.
Guesser:	
¿Es útil?	Is it useful?

When the player has found out what the object is, the one who answered the last question goes out of the room to be "It."

CARACOLES

(Caracoles is an expression like "Ha," literally *snails.)*

Any number may play this counting game.

The group first counts in unison, as far as they wish.

Uno, dos, tres, cuatro, cinco, etc.

Then the Leader explains that the counting will be repeated and when a number can be divided by three, all must add the word *caracoles* in unison, thus:

Uno, dos, tres, caracoles . . .   One, two, three, ha.

The game continues, with the group counting as far as they wish in unison.

✻   ✻   ✻   ✻   ✻

The game may be played with the individual players counting in rotation, and the appropriate player must add *caracoles* if his number is divisible by three. If the player fails to say *caracoles,* he is eliminated from the game and the counting goes on until one is left, who is declared the winner.

The game may be made even more challenging by requiring *caracoles* to be added after all multiples of three and all numbers containing a three. Other versions require *caracoles* after multiples of four, or some other number, according to the Leader's option.

NOMBRES DE LUGAR

(Place names)

Any number can play.

Needed: A large map of the Americas.

The first player locates a city on the map, points to it, and says:

Voy a Lima (Caracas, etc.)   I'm going to Lima (Caracas . . .)

The next player must repeat the name of the city in the following sentence:

Voy a Lima a comprar un   I'm going to Lima to buy a book.
libro. (or some other
noun beginning with the
same letter as the city).

If he does so correctly, he can locate the next city. If he fails to do so, the next player tries and the game goes on around the class. In each case the name of the place must be paired with a noun that begins with the same letter.

¿DONDE ESTA LA MUÑEQUITA?

(Where is the little doll?)

Any number may play.

Needed: A tiny doll, an inch or two in size.

As in other "seeking" games, one player is sent from the room and the object is hidden. In this instance, it is easier (and, some think, more fun) to hide so tiny an object: behind someone's ear, in an envelope, in the corner of a picture, etc.

The Leader asks:

¿Dónde está la muñequita?   Where is the little doll?

The player guesses:

Está sobre el escritorio.   It is on the desk.
or
Está en el sobre.   It is in the envelope.

The player gets three guesses to find the doll. If he guesses correctly, he gets the next turn to hide the doll. Players take turns being "It."

BOLICHES

(Bowling)

Up to 40 may play.

Needed: Small bowling pins, with numbers up to 10 marked on them with a felt pen. A ball.

The pins are set at a distance agreed upon. Players take turns sending the ball toward the pins. The player's score is registered by adding the numbers on the pins he knocks down. The group adds each player's score aloud, in this manner:

Jorge—cinco y siete son doce.	George, 5 and 7 are 12.
Manuel—nueve, dos y tres son catorce.	Manuel, 9, 2, and 3 are 14.
Ana—un estrike—cincuenta y cinco.	Ana, strike, 55.

The game continues in this way for each player in turn.

UN JUEGO CON EL MAPA

(A game with the map)

Any number may play.

Needed: A map of the world. A list of names of languages in Spanish.

Two students stand before a map of the world while the others in the group observe. The first says:

¿Quiere usted indicarme un	Will you show me a country
país de habla española?	that speaks Spanish?
(inglesa, italiana,	(English, Italian,
portuguesa, or some other	Portuguese)
adjective of nationality)	

The second student indicates a Spanish-speaking country in the world, with this sentence:

Aquí está Venezuela. Se	Here is Venezuela. Spanish
habla español.	is spoken.

The student must answer his questioner, in each case, with the name of a country where the language mentioned in the question is spoken. If he cannot do so, he sits down and someone else takes his place. If he answers correctly, he asks the next student the question, and the game proceeds in this manner.

COLECCION EN DEDAL

(Collection in a thimble)

Several teams or a number of partners may play.

Needed: A large thimble for each group or pair.

The players look for tiny objects, within a given time, that will fit into their thimbles. Out-of-doors objects might be seeds, small flowers, shells. Indoor objects might be buttons, pins, a piece of chalk, etc. At the end of the time limit, each group or pair must name each object in the thimble in Spanish in order to score.

Adapted from *Libro de juegos,* page 15. Permission to reprint granted by the World Bureau Office of the World Association of Girl Guides and Girl Scouts, New York City.

SUBIENDO LAS ESCALERAS

(Going up the ladders)

A good blackboard game for about 20 players in two teams.

The players are divided into two teams and each member has a turn writing a word and "climbing" his team's ladder as quickly as possible. The whole group decides on the kind of words to be written, for example, a word containing a certain letter of the alphabet, colors, articles of clothing, etc. The team filling the spaces on the ladder correctly in the shortest time is the winner. When both ladders have been filled in, the group may take turns using the words in sentences. Then another category of words may be chosen for another round. A model of the ladders, in which the words must contain the letter ñ, might look like this:

Escalera 1
6. soñar
5. España
4. mañana
3. niño
2. baño
1. señora

Escalera 2
5. sueño
4. español
3. año
2. enseñar
1. niña

¿QUIENES SABEN NADAR?

(Who knows how to swim?)

Two teams of players are used.

The game is played like a spelldown in two teams. The Leader reads or writes on the blackboard a list of words, one by one, beginning, for example, with *el perro*. The first player on the first team must answer:

El perro sabe nadar.	The dog knows how to swim.
or	
El perro no sabe nadar.	The dog doesn't know how to swim.

If the player fails to answer within a given time, or answers incorrectly, he is out of the game. Then a player on the other team tries to answer. The list consists of the names of living beings, *el perro* (dog), *el gato* (cat), *el pájaro* (bird), *el nene* (baby), *el maestro* (teacher), or even proper names of students, if desired. The Leader should start with words that are more familiar and go on to those less well-known. At the end of the game, the team with the most players left standing is the winner.

VAMOS A VIAJAR

(Let's take a trip)

Up to 40 may play the game in two relay teams.

Needed: Two large maps of Latin America. Two ribbons or strings. A card or paper for each player on which are written the names of two Latin American cities, such as *Quito—Panamá, Lima—Caracas,* etc.

Each player in turn goes to his team's map and connects his two cities with the ribbon or string as quickly as he can. He calls out the names as he does so. If he cannot find the cities on the map within a set time, or if he mispronounces the names, he returns to his place, and another takes his place. The team which finishes all its cards first is the winner.

The game may be played in the same manner with large maps of Europe, and the cards have names of cities in Spain paired with cities of other countries of Europe.

LAS ESTATUAS

(The statues)

As many as 40 may play.

Needed: A variety of objects familiar to the group.

The players line up in two teams, perhaps a boys' and a girls' team, and each one holds some object in his hand. Each team chooses one of its members to be the *estatua* (statue), to stand a short distance from the teams. At a signal from the Leader, the first player on one team runs to the *estatua,* places her in the position desired (a scout gazing into the distance, a dancer in a pose, or anything the team wishes). The first player holds up the object in her hand, gives the Spanish word for it, and places it somewhere about the *estatua,* in her hand, on her head, on the ground, etc.

Then a player from the other team takes a turn and does likewise with his team's *estatua.* He may put a hat on the *estatua's* head, a bunch of flowers in his hand, in an effort to make the *estatua* look funny. He must also name the object in Spanish.

If a player forgets or mispronounces the name of the article, one point is charged against his team. The next player on the other team makes the correction, with help from his team if necessary. The game continues with players taking turns. The Leader keeps score and announces the winning team. The game can be hilarious.

EL CUERPO

(The body)

An even number may play, in two teams.

One line of players faces the other, and a player from one team says:

| *Este es mi dedo—uno, dos,* | This is my finger—one, two, |
| *tres, cuatro* (up to ten). | three, four, etc. |

Before he reaches ten, a player on the opposite side must point to another part of the body, such as his ear, and say:

| *Esta es mi oreja—uno, dos,* | This is my ear—one, two, |
| *tres, cuatro* . . . | three, four . . . |

Another player on the first team must be ready to speak before the second player counts to ten, and the game continues in this manner through both teams. A player who fails to answer in time must drop out and the winning team is the one with more players remaining at the end of the game.

OBSERVACION DENTRO DEL CIRCULO

(Looking within the circle)

Two teams play this game, which is often played by Girl Scouts in Spanish-speaking countries.

Needed: A cord or rope, a number of small objects whose names are familiar to players.

A circle is formed with the rope and, while the players turn their backs, the Leader places several (5 or 6) of the objects within the circle. Both teams are then permitted 15 seconds to observe the objects. They turn their backs on the circle again and each team lists the names of the objects seen, as many as they can remember. The Spanish words for each must be used. One point is scored for the team for each article correctly listed. The game can be repeated for several rounds, using a different collection of objects each time. The team with the most points is the winner.

From *Libro de juegos,* page 11. Permission to reprint granted by the World Bureau Office of the World Association of Girl Guides and Girl Scouts, New York City.

TIRO AL BLANCO

(Target practice)

The entire class may play the game, as individuals or as teams.

Needed: A heavy piece of corrugated cardboard cut in a circle, and marked out like this:

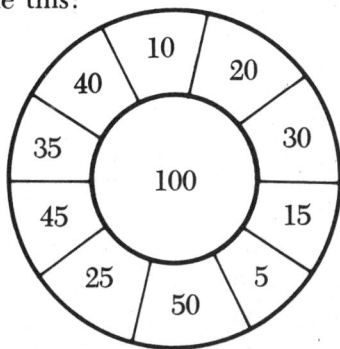

The target is placed on the floor about ten feet away from the players. Players take turns tossing a checker, bottle top, or similar object at the target. Each player must call out in Spanish the number he has scored. If he forgets it or mispronounces it, he gets no score. Any player who scores a bull's-eye is given another turn. One player acts as scorekeeper. Teams might like to have names, such as *Los Zorros* (Foxes) and *Los Lobos* (Wolves). At the end of play, the scorekeeper may announce:

¡Los Zorros ganaron!   The Foxes won!

LAS CANASTAS

(The baskets)

Two relay teams of ten persons each may play. This is a good exercise for graceful posture.

Needed: Two lightweight baskets, deep enough to hold three or four objects. Put different objects in each basket, such as fruit, flowers.

The two teams line up in two files. The first player on the first team picks up the objects for the basket, and says:

En mi canasta hay tres naranjas y una toronja. (or whatever the objects are)	In my basket there are 3 oranges and a grapefruit.

The first player on the other team also names the objects for his basket:

En mi canasta hay dos limones, una manzana y flores.	In my basket there are two lemons, an apple, and flowers.

Each player puts the objects in the basket and sets the basket on his head. Each starts out in the direction of a prearranged goal, trying to walk so that the basket does not fall from his head. Each must return to the starting point and give the basket to another one from his team, who likewise has to carry it the distance of the course. If the basket falls, the player must stop and balance it again before he goes on. The team which finishes first is the winner.

LA ESCALERA

(The staircase)

This game may be played by two teams or by individual students.

Have the students draw a staircase on their papers, with an object or an animal on the top step. Write the Spanish word for the animal, thus:

el gato

In order to score, one point for each step in the stair, students must write a Spanish word beginning with the same initial letter as the word at the top. For example, if the word *gato* is used, all words must begin with *g, gorra, grande, grano,* etc. When the time is up, students read their lists aloud.

Another version:

Draw a descending staircase with a ferocious animal at the bottom. In order to "escape" from the animal, and score points, students must write on each step a word that begins with the same initial letter before members of the other team can count to 20, 30, 40, or whatever number they choose, in Spanish. If the student fails to "escape" in the time allowed, he is out of the game. The staircase might look like this:

el tigre

Instead of drawing an animal or object, tell the students they must fill each step with a Spanish word containing a certain letter, such as *ll, ch, rr, ñ,* etc. Or have the steps filled with words in subject-matter categories, such as parts of the body, furniture, colors, etc.

OBSERVACION CASUAL

(Casual observation)

Any number may play.

Needed: A table, cloth, and a number of objects such as a coin, pin, book, pen, etc.

When the players enter the room, a number of small objects will be seen on the table but the Leader will make no mention of them. In the middle of the session, the Leader will cover the table with a cloth and the players must write the names of as many objects as they can recall. The one with the longest list of Spanish words correctly written is the winner. For those with less knowledge of Spanish, the objects on the table may be identified by a tag with the name printed in Spanish. Possible objects are:

una moneda	a coin
un lápiz	a pencil
un libro	a book
una plumafuente	a fountain pen
un pañuelo	a handkerchief
un cuaderno	a notebook
etc.	

EL ARBOL DE LOS NUMEROS

(The tree of numbers)

An individual or a group may play.

A large tree is drawn on the blackboard. At the end of each branch is a box containing the word for a number, as here:

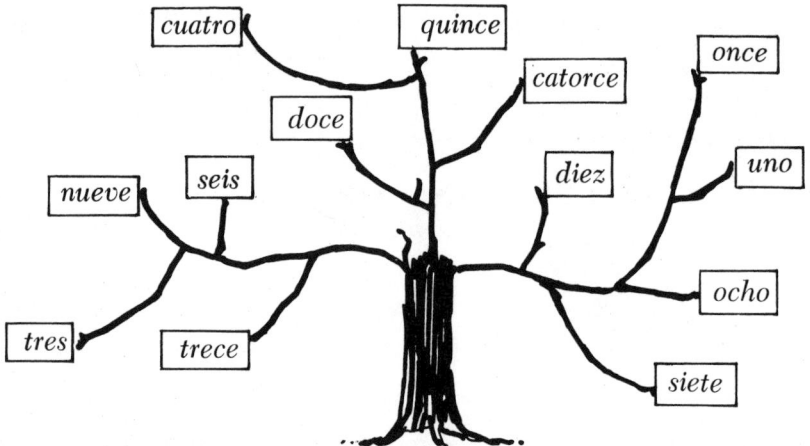

The object of the game is to see who can add the total of the leaves most quickly and accurately. The class may be divided into teams for a contest for the best mathematician in the class. The teacher changes the numbers of the leaves as the game proceeds, to see who can reach the new total first.

Another variation is to have the class find the total of the leaves and then, by erasing the numbers one by one, ascertain the new total.

COMBINACIONES MATEMATICAS
(Mathematical combinations)

This is an easy game for an individual or a group.

The object of the game is to make as many mathematical combinations of a pre-chosen number as possible within a specified time limit. Each player lists his combinations on a sheet of paper as quickly and accurately as possible. At the end of the time limit, each player must then read aloud in Spanish his list of combinations. Then a new number is chosen.

If the number chosen were 10, the following combinations might be listed:

	Read aloud:
2 + 8 = 10	*Dos y ocho son diez.*
20 − 10 = 10	*Veinte menos diez son diez.*
5 × 2 = 10	*Cinco por dos son diez.*
11 − 1 = 10	*Once menos uno son diez.*
3 + 7 = 10	*Tres y siete son diez.*
90 − 80 = 10	*Noventa menos ochenta son diez.*
etc.	

¿QUE COSA SE CAYO?
(What fell?)

About 35 may play.

Needed: About 10 objects that can be dropped without breaking, and a carton for them. Suggested objects: *un cuchillo* (knife), *dos tenedores* (two forks), *tres cucharas* (three spoons), *un zapato* (shoe), etc.

The players turn their backs and listen as the Leader takes each article from the carton and drops it to the floor. To introduce the players to the game, the Leader may drop a knife, and say:

El número uno.   Number one.
¿Se cayó . . . un tenedor?   Did a fork, spoon, or knife fall?
una cuchara?— un cuchillo?

The players list opposite 1 on their papers the name of the object they believe was dropped. The Leader proceeds with another object, each time naming several choices for what was dropped. At the end of the game, the players turn around and face the Leader with their lists. Quickly the Leader repeats the dropping of the articles, now seen, naming aloud each object so that players may check their lists. The one with the most correct answers wins. The game may also be played with oral answers instead of written ones.

LOS CUADROS

(The squares)

Two teams of from five to ten persons each.

Needed: A good-sized rectangle drawn on the floor, like this:

4	5
3	6
2	7
1	8

Any object that can be thrown easily, such as a beanbag, a checker, or a ring top.

Two teams are designated. Each player takes a turn pitching the beanbag into the square. As the beanbag falls on a number, all the players call out the number. A scorekeeper lists the score by teams and, at the end of the game, calls out the name of the winning team. All players may add the score aloud, if desired.

NOMBRE-ACROSTICO

(Name-acrostic)

Any number can play.

Each student chooses a Spanish name and writes the letters of it in a vertical column, one letter to a line. Within a time limit, he must now write a Spanish word on each line, using a letter of the name as the initial letter of each word. A model name and its acrostic might be:

A *Arbol*

L *Libro*

F *Fruta*

R *Ratón*

E *Elefante*

D *Dedo*

O *Oreja*

ESCOJO...

(I choose . . .)

Here is a good vocabulary review game for the whole class.

Show the class a picture containing a number of identifiable objects. Each player looks at the picture and makes three choices. He then writes each of them in the Spanish sentence:

Escojo . . . (la bicicleta).   I choose . . . (the bicycle).

Each player must write three sentences based on the picture. The pictures may be of random objects or of articles all within a given category, such as food, clothing, etc.

MI SECRETO

(My secret)

Up to 30 may play this guessing game.

Needed: An 8 x 10 piece of cardboard or stiff paper for each player.

Each player writes on his cardboard the title, *Mi secreto*, listing a few clues below it. He shows his card to the other players and reads aloud the clues, for example:

Mi Secreto	My Secret
Es pequeño.	It is small.
Es blanco.	It is white.
Es simpático.	It is likeable.
Es inteligente.	It is intelligent.
¿Qué es?	What is it?

Those in the group take turns guessing what it is. The one who guesses correctly then takes his card with its *secreto* and shows it to the group. If no one guesses the secret of the first player, he turns the card over and shows the group his secret, for example, *mi perro* (my dog).

III Projects for Individual Students or Groups

CAJAS DEL TESORO

(Treasure boxes)

Students learning the Spanish alphabet may enjoy this activity.

Collect empty shoe boxes and make a series of "treasure boxes." Each box will represent a letter of the Spanish alphabet. Within each box are collected small objects or pictures of objects whose names contain the letter in question.

For example, in the box marked *ch* there might be a picture of a boy, labelled *muchacho, chocolate,* etc. In the box marked *ñ* might be a *muñeca* (doll), a *niño, señor,* a picture of a sleeping child with *sueño,* and many others. The object of the game is to have members identify the "pieces of treasure."

The boxes may be constructed like a card file, with the words to be learned, together with an illustrative picture, listed on index cards and placed in the box for reference. If desired, a card may be discarded when it is agreed that the word or expression is familiar to everyone, and other cards may be added as new words are introduced.

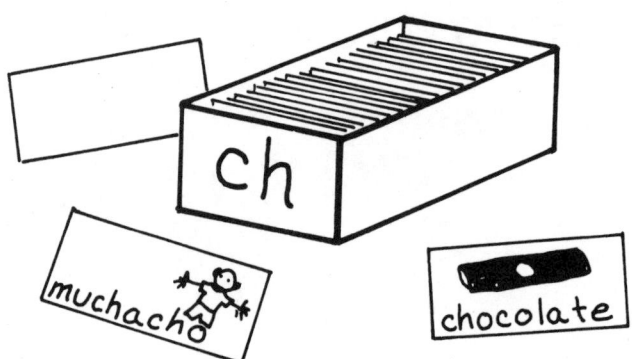

MIS LLAVES DORADAS

(My golden keys)

Draw keys on stiff, heavy paper and cut them out. They may be sprayed with gold paint, if desired. With a felt pen, write on each key a "good manners" expression. Punch a hole in each key and put the keys together on a metal ring for an attractive decoration for blackboard or wall. Expressions that may be written on the keys are:

Gracias	Thank you
Por favor	Please
Hágame el favor	If you please
¿Me hace usted el favor?	Will you please?
Con permiso	With your permission
Tenga la bondad	Please
Dispénseme	Excuse me
No hay de que	You're welcome
Perdón usted	Pardon me
De nada	You're welcome
or any others desired.	

EL JARDIN ZOOLOGICO

(The zoo)

Children in grades K-3 will enjoy making a Spanish zoo.

Cages for the zoo can be made by fixing lollipop sticks or toothpicks around the edges of the desired number of paper plates. Small figures of animals or cutouts are placed inside each cage and signs are made and set before each cage, reading *el oso* (the bear), *los monos* (the monkeys), *el elefante* (the elephant), etc.

LA FAMILIA SANCHEZ

(The Sanchez family)

From light-colored or white felt, cut four figures: a father, mother, son, and daughter. From various colored scraps of felt, cut articles of clothing for each member of the family. Mount the figures on a felt board and let members of the class take turns putting the various articles of clothing on the family, using the Spanish names for the clothing in sentences as they do so, such as:

El señor Sánchez lleva los pantalones azules.	Mr. Sanchez is wearing blue trousers.
Luisa tiene la falda amarilla.	Luisa has a yellow skirt.

Articles may be labelled with Spanish names. Let students look up words for articles of clothing that they wish to put on the members of the family.

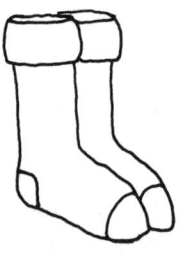

los calcetines

el sombrero

los pantalones

los zapatos

LA CASA SANCHEZ

(The Sanchez' house)

la mesa

la cama

el sofá

la sala *el comedor*

While the class is learning the parts of the house, let a group of students furnish a doll house, using doll furniture in the various rooms and putting small figures of a model family in the house.

Each room of the house may be labelled in Spanish, and the articles of furniture may also be marked with their Spanish names. The house can provide material for oral conversation and question-and-answer drill, as the class tries to name the pieces of furniture in each room or locate the members of the family.

¿QUE TIEMPO HACE?

(How is the weather?)

Make a "weather board" from a flannel board. A round piece of yellow felt may be cut out for a sunny day, a piece of gray felt to represent clouds, or a piece of gray with white chalk marks for rain. Along with each felt picture is a sign describing the weather condition, such as *"Hace sol"* (It is sunny).

When the "weather board" is finished, students can take turns keeping it up to date each day by mounting the appropriate symbol and sign on it.

EL CALENDARIO

(The calendar)

Students might like to make a large calendar for the wall, marked with the Spanish name for the month at the top and with the days of the week printed in Spanish above the numbers. Make the number spaces large enough so that the weather conditions can be written under each day. Important dates for the class may also be indicated in Spanish on the calendar. Different students may undertake to make the calendar for each month of the school year. The calendar for December might be modelled on this one:

Diciembre						
Domingo	Lunes	Martes	Miércoles	Jueves	Viernes	Sábado
1	2	3	4	5	6	7
8	9	10	11	12	13	14
15	16	17	18	19	20	21
22	23	24	25	26	27	28
29	30	31				

VAMOS A HACER
UN CUADERNO ESPECIAL

(Let's make a special notebook)

Students may enjoy combining a special interest and their study of Spanish vocabulary. Notebooks or scrapbooks might be made, with pictures labelled in Spanish. Some subjects might be:

1. *Los deportes* (Sports).

2. *Mi familia* (My family). Pictures of the student and the members of his family might be accompanied by a brief description of the person.

Mi papá. Es alto. Es bueno.   My Dad. He is tall. He is good.

3. *Mis amigos* (My friends). Snapshots of friends will have appropriate descriptive comments.

4. *Los animales* (The animals).

5. *Mi pueblo* (My town). Draw pictures or maps of places of interest in town.

6. *Las modas* (Fashions). Girls will enjoy making a notebook of fashions at the same time that they learn valuable vocabulary.

7. *Mi casa* (My house). Draw rooms or use photographs. How many things in the house can you label?

LA LOTERIA
(Lottery)

Lottery, or Bingo or Lotto as it is called in the United States is very popular in the small towns of Mexico. No special materials are needed to play American-style Bingo in Spanish, but students might enjoy making *Lotería* cards such as are used in the villages south of the border. The cards have pictures of animals, flowers, musical instruments, or even Death and the Devil. Players cover the pictures that are called with *frijoles* (beans) and call out "*Lotería, ¡ lo tengo!*" when they have filled the appropriate number of spaces.

Students can make their own *Lotería* cards of stiff cardboard, putting numbers on one side if they wish (for Bingo), and filling the squares on the reverse side with pictures cut from magazines or newspapers. The Leader's card should, of course, be large enough to have spaces for all the numbers in sequence on one side, and all the pictures on the other. Players' cards will have only part of the numbers and pictures and no two cards should be exactly the same. Small pieces of cardboard should be made for all the numbers and all the pictures. Buttons, bottle caps, or circles or squares of cardboard may be used for marking the players' cards.

LOS LETREROS
(The signs)

With cardboard and felt pens students can letter signs such as would be found in Spanish-speaking countries. The words that appear on the signs may be found in photographs in Spanish books and in magazines and newspapers from Spanish-speaking countries. After the signs have been made, students can find in magazines pictures that are illustrative of the individual signs, fasten the signs to the pictures, and hang them around the classroom. Some of the signs might say:

Se prohibe anunciar	No advertising
¡Alto!	Stop!
Refrescos	Refreshments
Se alquila	For rent
Aquí se habla español	Spanish is spoken here
Se prohibe estacionar	No parking
Se prohibe fumar	No smoking

or others that students may know.

EL CAMINO
(The road)

On a small table, set toy automobiles and houses to represent city streets or highways. Make signs with road directions in Spanish and place them at appropriate places in the streets. Some of the directions for the signs may be:

Cuidado con el tren	Watch for train
Desviación	Detour
Velocidad Máxima	Maximum Speed
Despacio	Slow
Curva	Curve
Alto	Stop

Precaución	Caution
Tome la derecha	Go to the right
Escuela	School

LA PIÑATA

Since the traditional *piñata* of Mexico has become so popular at children's parties in the United States, students would enjoy making their own *piñata* for a Christmas party, or even for another festive occasion.

The *piñata* is traditionally made of earthenware or papier maché, but students can use a lightweight cardboard box or a paper bag. This is decorated with crepe paper according to the taste of the children, and is filled with candies and fruit and tied or fastened at the top. Students with creative imagination can make the *piñata* to resemble a bird, an airplane, a burro, or anything they wish.

The finished *piñata* is hung out of reach of the children. Each child is blindfolded in turn and, with a long stick, tries to break the *piñata* so that the sweets cascade out. As each child takes a turn, the other players call out: *"¡Dale!"* (Hit it!). Since there is always a wild scramble for the candies and nuts, it is well for them to be wrapped individually to avoid their being damaged.

JINCANAS

For a party, students might like to make *jincanas,* the party favors that are used in children's parties in Lima, Peru. *Jincanas* are small gifts or treats, such as candy, cookies, little toys, feathers, rice, or confetti, wrapped individually in bright-colored paper and strung on a line just out of reach. Each child is blindfolded and given a chance to knock down one of the *jincanas* with a stick. One *jincana* is always left empty, according to tradition.

From *Hi Neighbor,* Book 6, United States Committee for UNICEF, Hastings House Publishers, New York. Permission to reprint granted by publisher.

EL CUERPO

(The body)

Match the words in the list below with the body in the picture, by drawing a line to the part that corresponds to the word:

1. *la boca*   6. *los brazos*

2. *la nariz*   7. *la mano*

3. *la cabeza*   8. *los dedos*

4. *el pie*   9. *las orejas*

5. *los ojos*   10. *la pierna*

¿QUE FALTA?
(What is missing?)

Match each sentence below to the person that it correctly describes by drawing a line from the sentence to that person's picture.

1. *Falta la boca.*

2. *Falta una oreja.*

3. *Falta un ojo.*

4. *Faltan los pies.*

5. *Falta un dedo.*

6. *Falta la cabeza.*

7. *Falta un brazo.*

8. *Faltan las manos.*

9. *Falta una pierna.*

10. *Falta la nariz.*

¿QUIENES SON?
(Who are they?)

Draw a line from one of the words in the list to the person in the picture whom it names.

1. *El nené*   6. *El niño*

2. *El enfermo*   7. *La niña*

3. *El aviador*   8. *El mesero*

4. *El médico*   9. *El campesino*

5. *La abuela*   10. *El carpintero*

¿QUIENES FALTAN?

(Who are missing?)

Answer the following questions, telling whether or not the person is missing from the picture. Model: *¿Falta el padre? Sí, falta el padre. No, no falta el padre.*

1. *¿Falta el enfermo?* _____

2. *¿Falta el campesino?* _____

3. *¿Falta el aviador?* _____

4. *¿Falta el nené?* _____

5. *¿Falta la niña?* _____

6. *¿Falta el mesero?* _____

7. *¿Falta el carpintero?* _____

LA CASA RIDICULA

(The ridiculous house)

A. *La casa está toda desarreglada.*   The house is disorderly.

Answer the questions based on the picture:

1. *¿Dónde está el sofá?* _____

2. *¿Dónde está la cama?* _____

3. *¿Dónde están las flores?* _____

4. *¿Quién está a la puerta?* _____

5. *¿Quién está cazando el gato?* _____

B. *Voy a arreglar la casa.*   I'm going to straighten up the house.

Complete the following statements:

1. *Voy a poner el sofá en* _____

2. *Voy a poner la mesa en* _____

3. *Voy a poner las flores en* _____

4. *Voy a poner el tigre en* _____

5. *Voy a poner la cama en* _____

C. *La casa está en orden.*   The house is in order.

Complete the following sentences:

1. *La mesa está en* _____

2. *La cama está en* _____

3. *El elefante se fue a* _____

4. *El gato está* _____

5. *El sofá está en* _____

LOS NUMEROS RIMADOS
(Rhymed numbers)

Each of the words or expressions in the following list rhymes with a Spanish number. Can you list beside each word a number that rhymes with it? Each number should be a different one.

mes	*dámelos*
los	*a la vez*
llueve	*vete*
la renta	*teatro*
bizcocho	*bronce*

ANSWERS

LOS NUMEROS RIMADOS: 3 *(tres)*; 2 *(dos)*; 9 *(nueve)*; 40 *(cuarenta)*; 8 *(ocho)*; 22 *(veintidós)*; 23 *(veintitrés)*; 7 *(siete)*; 4 *(cuatro)*; 11 *(once)*.

¿CUANTO?
(How much?)

These are some of the kinds of problems found in Spanish arithmetic books. Students may enjoy testing both reading and mathematical skill with them.

1. *Tengo seis manzanas. Le doy dos a Jorge. ¿Cuántas me quedan?*

2. *En una clase con 22 alumnos presentes, hay 4 ausentes. ¿De cuántos alumnos consta la clase entera?*

3. *Si un libro cuesta cinco dólares, ¿cuánto cuesta:*

    1) *la media docena?*
    2) *la docena?*
    3) *el ciento?*

4. *Cuenta de 2 en 2 hasta una docena.*

5. *Cuenta de 2 en 2 hasta veinte.*

6. *45 alumnos y 5 maestros van en excursión al museo. Si cada maestro va acompañado del mismo número de alumnos, ¿cuántos grupos hay y cuántos alumnos hay en cada grupo?*

7. *Mi mamá me envió a la tienda con tres dólares, a comprar comestibles. Después de comprar:*

> *una docena de huevos @ .67*
> *una libra de carne @ .48*
> *una libra de queso @ .75*
> *dos libras de frijoles @ .25 la libra*
> *¿cuánto dinero me quedó?*

ANSWERS

¿CUANTO?: 1) 4; 2) 26; 3) 30, 60, 500; 4) 2, 4, 6, 8, 10, 12; 5) 2, 4, 6, 8, 10, 12, 14, 16, 18, 20; 6) *5 grupos de 9 alumnos cada uno;* 7) *60 centavos.*

¿SE ACUERDA USTED DE ESTOS CUENTOS?

(Do you remember these stories?)

Read the sentences based on familiar stories, and check *VERDAD* or *NO ES VERDAD*, according to whether the statement is true or false.

I. LOS TRES OSOS

(The Three Bears)

VERDAD·NO ES VERDAD

1. *El oso grande dijo –Sí, mamá, la sopa está caliente. Vamos a dar un paseo por el bosque.* _____ _____

2. *El oso pequeño dijo –Sí, papá,*
la sopa está caliente. Vamos
a dar un paseo por el bosque.   _____   _____

3. *Los tres osos fueron a la playa.*   _____   _____

4. *Mientras los tres osos estaban*
afuera, la Niña Goldilocks
entró en la casa.   _____   _____

5. *La Niña Goldilocks dijo –¡Ay!*
¡Esta sopa está caliente!   _____   _____

6. *La Niña Goldilocks se comió*
toda la sopa del oso grande.   _____   _____

7. *Ella se acostó en el sofá.*   _____   _____

8. *Ella se fue corriendo de la*
casa de los tres osos.   _____   _____

ANSWERS   1. f; 2. t; 3. f; 4. t; 5. t; 6. f; 7. f; 8. t.

II. CAPEPUCITA ROJA
(Little Red Ridinghood)

VERDAD · NO ES VERDAD

1. *Caperucita Roja fue a visitar*
a su abuelo.   _____   _____

2. *La abuela vivía en el bosque.*   _____   _____

3. *Caperucita Roja no llevó nada*
a su abuela.   _____   _____

4. *El lobo era muy amistoso.*   _____   _____

5. *Caperucita Roja dijo –¡Qué*
ojos tan grandes tienes, abuelo!   _____   _____

6. *El leñador mató al lobo.*   _____   _____

ANSWERS   1. f; 2. t; 3. f; 4. f; 5. f; 6. t.

III. LA GALLINITA ROJA

(The Little Red Hen)

VERDAD · NO ES VERDAD

1. *Había una vez una gallinita roja que tenía tres pollitos.* _____ _____

2. *Vivían cerca de un cerdo, un perro y un gato.* _____ _____

3. *Un día la gallinita halló un grano de maíz.* _____ _____

4. *El cerdo, el perro y el gato le dijeron -Vamos a ayudarte.* _____ _____

5. *El cerdo, el perro y el gato sembraron el grano.* _____ _____

6. *La gallinita roja dijo —¿Quién quiere ayudarme a comer el pan?* _____ _____

7. *La gallinita roja se comió todo el pan.* _____ _____

ANSWERS   1. t; 2. t; 3. f; 4. f; 5. f; 6. t; 7. f.

IV. EL MUÑEQUITO DE PAN

(The Gingerbread Boy)

VERDAD · NO ES VERDAD

1. *De la masa la vieja cortó un muñequito en forma de muchacho.* _____ _____

2. *—Este muñequito de pan será hijo para nosotros– dijo la vieja.* _____ _____

3. *El muñequito de pan saltó
   del horno.*   _____   _____

4. *El muñequito de pan dijo
   —Señor, perro. Me escapé de los
   viejos; me escapé del muchacho,
   pero no pude escaparme de ti.*   _____   _____

5. *El muñequito de pan llegó a la
   orilla de un río ancho.*   _____   _____

6. *El zorro dijo –Si quieres, te llevo
   a través del lago.*   _____   _____

7. *El muñequito se escapó del zorro,
   pero no se escapó del gato.*   _____   _____

ANSWERS   1. t; 2. f; 3. t; 4. f; 5. t; 6. f; 7. f.

V. EL POLLITO
(Chicken Little)

VERDAD·NO ES VERDAD

1. *El pollito dijo —Parece que el
   cielo se está cayendo.*   _____   _____

2. *El pollito echó a correr.*   _____   _____

3. *La gallinita preguntó —¿Cómo
   sabes que se está cayendo?*   _____   _____

4. *El gallo preguntó —¿Cómo
   sabes que se está cayendo?*   _____   _____

5. *El pollito dijo —Lo vi con mis
   propios oídos.*   _____   _____

6. *El pollito dijo —Lo oí con mis
   propios ojos.*   _____   _____

ANSWERS   1. t; 2. t; 3. t; 4. t; 5. f; 6. f.

LOS CUENTOS

(Stories)

These questions are based on six familiar stories: *"Los Tres Osos," "Caperucita Roja," "La Gallinita Roja," "El Muñequito de Pan," "El Pollito,"* and *"Cenicienta."* Which character from the stories said each of the following statements?

1. *¿Quieres llevar esta canasta a tu abuela? Cuidado, porque en la canasta hay fruta y una torta.* _____

   _____

2. *¡Alguien ha entrado aquí y se ha tomado toda mi sopa!*

   _____

3. *Parece que el cielo se está cayendo. ¿Que haré?* _____

   _____

4. *Miren ustedes, un grano de trigo. Si lo siembro, tendremos trigo para pan. ¿Me ayudan?* _____

   _____

5. *¡Ajá! Te escapaste de los viejos; te escapaste del muchacho; te escapaste del perro; te escapaste del gato; pero no puedes escaparte de mí.* _____

6. *—Quieres asistir al baile, ¿verdad?* _____

   _____

ANSWERS

1. *La madre de Caperucita* (Red Ridinghood's mother)
2. *El oso pequeño* (The little bear)
3. *Pollito* (Chicken Little)
4. *La gallinita roja* (The little red hen)
5. *El zorro* (The fox to the gingerbread boy)
6. *El hada madrina* (The fairy godmother, to Cinderella)

ADIVINANZAS

(Riddles)

1. *Oro no es, plata no es, adivina lo que es.*
2. *¿Qué tiene ojo y no ve?*
3. *Cuando chiquito, verdecito, y cuando grandecito, negrito.*
4. *¿Qué hay en medio del mar y no se moja?*
5. *Una niña vestida de verde, tiene el corazón colorado.*
6. *¿Qué hay en medio del sol y no se quema?*

ANSWERS

1) *el plátano (Plata no)*—the banana
2) *la aguja*—the needle
3) *el higo*—the fig
4) the *a* of *mar*
5) *la sandía*—the watermelon
6) the *o* of *sol*

IV Let's Put On a Spanish Program

EL BAILE DE LOS RATONCITOS

(The dance of the mice)

Characters: Announcer, Gato, eight *Ratoncitos.*

Needed: Gay dance music. Three signs: a picture of a cat labelled *"El Gato";* a house labelled *"La casa de don Tomás";* a picture of mice labelled *"Los Ratoncitos."*

(At one side of the stage is the sign *"La casa de don Tomás"* and on the other is the sign *"Los Ratoncitos.")*

Announcer (Pointing to appropriate sign):
Este es el gato.   This is the cat.
(The gato goes behind the sign *"La casa de don Tomás.")*

Announcer:
Estos son los ratoncitos.   These are the mice.
(Announcer shows sign *"Los Ratoncitos,"* and exits. Enter the *Ratoncitos,* in four couples, and step forward).

First Couple:
Somos ratoncitos.   We are mice.

Second Couple:
Que venimos a bailar.   Who came to dance.

Third Couple:
No más que venga el gato.   Just so the cat doesn't come.

Fourth Couple:
De la casa de don Tomás. From the house of don Tomas.
(Gay dance music begins and the four couples form a circle and dance around. Suddenly the *Gato* springs out from behind the sign and the *Ratoncitos* scatter.)

Ratoncitos (All together):
¡Ay! ¡No! ¡Señor Gato!	Oh, no! Mr. Cat!
¡Vamos!	Let's go!

(*Gato* pursues them offstage.)

SOMOS CABALLITOS
(We are little horses)

Characters: Announcer, leader of Caballitos. Other Caballitos.

Leader of Caballitos:
Somos caballitos.	We are little horses.

Announcer:
¿Qué quieren hacer?	What do you want to do?

Caballitos (together):
Queremos galopear. Vamos.	We want to gallop. Let's go.
(*Caballitos* go through motions of galloping, then stop.)	

Announcer:
¿A dónde van?	Where are you going?

Caballitos:
Vamos a nuestro pueblo.	We are going to our town.
Adiós. Adiós. Hasta la vista.	Goodbye. Goodbye. See you later.

(*Caballitos* gallop away.)

LA MERIENDA

(The tea party)

Characters: Five girls, a Hostess and four Guests.

Needed: Table, coffeepot, teapot, sugarbowl, creamer, cups and saucers, spoons, plate of cookies, chairs.

(The Hostess sits at the table. The Guests begin to arrive and the Hostess greets them).

Hostess:
Buenas tardes, Julia,   Good afternoon . . .
Rosa, etc.

Guests:
Buenas tardes, Lupe.

Hostess: (To Guest 1):
¿Cómo está usted?   How are you?

Guest 1:
Muy bien, gracias. ¿Y   Very well, thank you. And you?
usted?

Hostess:
Muy bien, gracias.

Guest 2:
¡Qué bonito vestido!   What a pretty dress!

Guest 3:
Hace calor, ¿verdad?   It's hot, isn't it?

(Other Guests say things that occur to them, or answer with "*Gracias*" or "*Sí.*" Slight hubbub as all sit.)

Hostess:
¿*Té?*   Tea?

Guest 1:
Sí, gracias, con limón.   Yes, thanks, with lemon.

Hostess:
¿*Té?*

Guest 2:
Sí, por favor, con leche.   Yes, please, with milk.

Hostess:
¿*Té?*

Guest 3:
No, gracias, prefiero café sólo.   No, thanks, I prefer black coffee.

Guest 4:
Café, por favor, con leche.   Coffee, please, with milk.

Hostess (passing cookies):
¿*Galletitas?*   Cookies?

All Guests:
Sí, gracias. Muchas gracias, etc.   Yes, thanks. Many thanks, etc.

LOS NIÑOS DESOBEDIENTES
(The disobedient children)

Characters: Five children (two boys and three girls), *Madre*, Shopkeeper.

Needed: A small table for a counter, on which are fruits, vege-
tables, articles of clothing. A broom. A market bag and shopping
list for *Madre.*

(The *Madre* and the children are at one side of the stage in
their house. At the other side is the shopkeeper standing behind
the counter. The *Madre* picks up a market bag and the shopping
list.)

Madre:

Voy a la tienda. Pórtense bien.	I'm going to the store. Be good.

Niños:

Sí, mamá. Adiós.	Yes, mama. Goodbye.

Madre (addressing each child in turn):

Tú, Paco, a barrer el piso.	Paco, sweep the floor.

(*Paco* goes through motions of sweeping.)

Tú, María, a lavar los platos.	María, wash the dishes.

(*María* pretends to wash dishes.)

Tú, Juan, a limpiar la casa.	Juan, clean the house.

(*Juan* cleans.)

Celia y Trina, a preparar la cena.	Celia and Trina, fix supper.

(*Celia* and *Trina* pretend to be preparing a meal.)

Paco:

Mamá, déjanos acompañarte.	Mama, let us go with you.

Madre:

No, niños, a trabajar.	No, children, get to work.

(*Madre* goes to other side of stage, to store.)

Shopkeeper:

Buenos días, señora Sánchez. ¿Cómo está usted?	Good day, Mrs. Sanchez. How are you?

Madre:
  Muy bien, gracias. ¿Y   Very well, thanks. And you?
  usted?

Shopkeeper:
  Bien, gracias. ¿En qué   Fine, thanks. How can I
  puedo ayudarle?   help you?

Madre:
  Pues, a ver. Naranjas,   Well, let's see. Half a dozen
  media docena . . .   oranges . . .

(*Madre* points to articles displayed. Shopkeeper picks them up as the *Madre* names them, and wraps them in sheets of newspaper.)

Madre:
  . . . un kilo de frijoles   . . . a kilo of beans . . .
  . . . esa cazuela . . . No, la   . . . that pot . . . No, the big
  cazuela grande . . .   pot . . .

(Meanwhile the *Niños* have left their work and stealthily approach the *Madre*. They come up in back of her and she appears to be unaware of their presence.)

Madre:
  . . . y una escoba . . .   . . . and a broom . . . for my . . .
  para mis . . .

(turning suddenly on *Niños*, the broom in her hand.)

¡niños desobedientes!   . . . disobedient children!
¡Váyanse a la casa!   Go home! Get going!
¡Váyanse!

(*Niños* run for home pursued by *Madre* with broom.)

EL FRUTERO

(The fruit seller)

Characters: Niños and *Frutero* (Fruit seller).

Needed: A basket, bananas, a pineapple, a papaya, mangos. (These could be cut out of cardboard.)

Niño 1:

El frutero del Sur.	The fruit seller from the South.
El frutero llegó.	The fruit seller has come.

Frutero: (Enters with basket of fruit.)

Nadie vende la fruta	No one sells fruit
Como la vendo yo.	As I sell it.

Niño 2:

Fruta del trópico quiero.	I want fruit from the tropics.
Nadie la puede encontrar.	No one can find it.

Niños (Together):

Piñas, papayas y mangos y plátanos llevarán.	Pineapple, papaya and mangos and bananas they will bring.
Piñas, papayas y mangos y plátanos llevarán.	

(The *frutero* indicates the fruits as they are named.)

Frutero:

¡Piñas! ¡Papayas! ¡Mangos! ¡Plátanos!
¡Piñas! ¡Papayas! ¡Mangos! ¡Plátanos!

Niños (speaking different lines all at once):

¿A cómo la piña?	How much is the pineapple?
Quiero dos mangos.	I want two mangos.
¿Cuánto valen los plátanos?	How much are bananas?
etc.	

From *The Forgotten Village*, by John Steinbeck, The Viking Press, New York, pages 32-3. Permission to reprint given by publishers.

EL PERICO

(The parrot)

Characters: Parrot seller, her daughter, *Niños.*

Needed: Several small paper parrots or pictures of parrots. A rose.

Parrot Seller:

Yo vendo mis periquitos, son finos y muy bonitos.	I sell my parrots, they are fine and pretty.
Los traigo desde Colima y vienen muy bien cuidados.	I bring them from Colima and they are very well taken care of.

Niños:

Daca, daca, daca, perico;	Give me . . . little parrot.
daca, daca, daca la pata.	Give me . . . your foot.

Parrot Seller:

¿Quién compra mis periquitos?	Who will buy my parrots?
Los vendo muy baratitos;	I sell them very cheap.
sus plumas son relucientes,	Their feathers are shiny.
su pico muy encorvado.	Their beaks very curved.

(Points to parrots' feathers and beaks as she speaks.)

Niños:

Pica, pica, pica, perico;	Peck . . . little parrot.
pica, pica, pica la rosa.	Peck . . . the rose.

(One of *niños* extends a rose toward the parrot.)

Parrot Seller:

Son finos mis periquitos; me quedan ya muy poquitos.	My parrots are fine; I have only a few left.
¡Ay, niña! llévese el suyo.	Child, take yours.

(Parrot Seller coaxes *niños*, one by one, to buy a parrot.)

Niños:
Daca, daca, daca, perico.
Daca, daca, daca la pata.

Daughter:
Mamita, suerte tuvimos;   Mama, we were lucky.
ya todo, todo vendimos.   We've sold them all.

Parrot Seller:
No queda ni un periquito,   Not a parrot left,
y mira, cuánto dinero.   and look how much money.

Niños:
Pica, pica, pica, perico;
pica, pica, pica la rosa.

From *El Cancionero de la Escuela y del Hogar*, by Leonardo Lis, Editorial Progreso, Mexico, D.F., Mexico, page 50. Permission to reprint granted by publisher.

EL MUSICO AMBULANTE

(The strolling musician)

Characters: Músico (musician), *Niños.*

Needed: Toy violin, guitar, flute, and drum.

Músico:
Soy músico ambulante, y sé   I am a strolling musician,
    cantar también;   and I can sing, too.
si quieren escucharme,   If you want to hear me I'll play
el violín les tocaré.   a violin for you.

Niños:
Sin e sun, sun, sun.
    (Repeat 3 more times.)
    (*Músico* and *Niños* pretend to play violin.)

Músico and Niños:
Mi pieza ya acabé.   I've finished my piece.
    (All put down violins in pantomime.)

Músico:

Soy músico ambulante, y sé cantar
también; si quieren escucharme, la guitarra
tocaré.

. . .

I'll play the guitar.

Niños:

Plin, plun, plin, plin, plin.
(Repeat 3 more times.)

Músico and Niños:

Mi pieza ya acabé.

Músico:

Soy músico ambulante, y sé cantar
también; si quieren escucharme, mi
flauta tocaré. I'll play my flute.

Niños:

Fi, fu, fi, fi, fi.
(Repeat 3 more times.)

Músico and Niños:

Mi pieza ya acabé.

Músico:

Soy músico ambulante, y sé cantar
también; si quieren escucharme,
el tambor les tocaré. I'll play the drum for you.

Niños:

Ra, ta, plan, plan, plan
(Repeat 3 more times.)
Músico and Niños:

Mi pieza ya acabé.

From *El Cancionero de la Escuela y del Hogar,* by Leonardo Lis, Editorial Progreso, Mexico, D.F., Mexico, page 50. Permission to reprint granted by publisher.

LOS CUENTOS REVUELTOS

(Scrambled stories)

Characters: Red Ridinghood's Grandmother and the Three Bears.

Needed: A blanket, a bench for a bed, a table.

(*Scene:* Grandmother's cabin. She is lying on the bed, covered by the blanket, asleep. Knock offstage.)

Abuela (Grandmother):

¿*Quién es?*	Who is it?

Voices offstage:

Los tres osos, a sus órdenes.	The three bears, at your service.

Abuela:

Ah, pasen, mis amigos.	Oh, come in, my friends.

(*Los tres osos* enter. The Big Bear is carrying a bunch of flowers.)

Osos:

Buenos días, abuela. Muy	Good day, grandmother.
buenos días. Buenos días.	Good day, good day.

Oso Grande (Big Bear):

¿*Cómo está usted, abuela?*	How are you, grandmother?

Abuela:

Muy contenta, gracias. Mi	Very happy, thanks. My
nieta, Caperucita, viene a	granddaughter, Red
visitarme hoy.	Ridinghood, is coming to
	visit today.

Osos:

Vaya. ¡Qué bueno!	Well. How nice. Fine.
¡*Magnífico!*	

(Mother Bear indicates the flowers.)

Oso Mediano (Middle Bear) :
  Las flores . . .   The flowers . . .

Oso Grande:
  ¿Las flores?   The flowers? . . . Oh, yes, the
  (Looks at them.)   flowers . . . They are for you,
  Ah, sí, las flores . . .   grandmother.
  Son para usted, abuela.
  (He puts the flowers on the table.)

Abuela:
  Gracias, mil gracias.   Thanks ever so much.

Oso Grande:
  Cogimos las flores en el   We picked the flowers in the
    bosque. Fuimos a dar un   woods. We went to take a
    paseo mientras se enfriaba   walk while the soup was
    la sopa.   cooling.

Oso Pequeño (Small Bear) :
  Sí, la sopa. Papá, tengo   Yes, the soup. Papa, I'm hungry.
    hambre.

Oso Mediano:
  Yo también tengo hambre.   I'm hungry, too.

Oso Grande:
  Yo también. Vamos a casa   Me, too. Let's go home and
    a desayunarnos.   have breakfast.

Osos:
  Adiós, abuela. Adiós.   Goodbye, grandmother.
  Hasta la vista.   See you again.
  Nuestros saludos a   Our regards to Red Ridinghood.
    Caperucita.

Abuela:
  Adiós. Adiós, amigos.   Goodbye, friends. May God be
    Vayan ustedes con Dios.   with you.

RIMAS PARA LOS NIÑOS
(Rhymes for young children)

This rhyme is said when someone rides a child on his knees:

Arre, caballito,	Get up, little horse,
vamos a Belén,	we're going to Bethlehem,
que mañana es fiesta,	for tomorrow is a holiday,
pasado también.	and the next day, too.

❖ ❖ ❖ ❖ ❖

In this "Pat-a-cake" rhyme children pretend they are making tortillas.

Tortilla, tortilla,	Tortilla . . .
para mamá.	for mother.
Tortilla, tortilla,	. . .
para papá.	for father.
Tortilla, tortilla,	. . .
para María.	for Maria.
Tortilla, tortilla,	. . .
para mi tía.	for my aunt.

❖ ❖ ❖ ❖ ❖

Children in chorus go through corresponding gestures while reciting this rhyme.

Estas son las manos,	These are my hands.
la la la la la la.	. . .
Estos son los pies,	These are my feet.
pla pla pla pla pla pla.	. . .

JUEGOS CON LOS DEDOS DE LAS MANOS

(Finger games)

These are rhymes to accompany finger games such as are played with very young children.

1. Both the child's hands are held together, palm to palm, and, as the rhyme is said, each pair of fingers, beginning with the little one, is indicated.

A la boda de éste y éste se convidan éste y éste, y éste le dice a éste que si éste no va con éste, no puede ir éste con éste.	To the wedding of this one and this one are invited this one and this one, and this one says to this one that if this one doesn't go with this one, this one can't go with this one.

2. In Spanish-speaking countries, this rhyme is the equivalent of "This Little Pig Went to Market." Spanish-speaking people start with the little finger in saying the rhyme.

Este se halló un huevito, éste lo quebró, éste lo frió, éste lo echó sal, y este viejo gordo se lo comió.	This one found a little egg, this one broke it, this one fried it, this one salted it, and this old fatty ate it up.

3. A rhyme that Spanish-speaking people recite while tickling a small child. As the rhyme is recited, the person's hand is moving from the child's hand up his arm to his side.

Tin, tin, la vaca pintada y el buey talentón; chorrito, chorrito, hasta que llegó al pocito.	(A nonsense rhyme in which a painted cow and an ox scurry to get to the well).

(From Revista del Folklore, Instituto Colombiano de Antropología, Segunda Epoca, Vol. I, II, 1952, page 127.)

LOS PATITOS
(The ducklings)

Los patitos, cui, cui, cui, *pasan todos por aquí.* *Pico, pico, pico, pico,* *adelante va el más chico.*	The little ducks, . . . all pass by here. Pico, . . . The smallest in the lead.

❄ ❄ ❄ ❄ ❄

Two rhymes about frogs.

Cu-cu, cantaba la rana. *Cu-cu, debajo del agua.*	Cu-cu sang the frog. Cu-cu, under the water.
Ranita, ranita, *contenta está.* *Salta y come y dice,* *"cua, cua."*	Little frog, little frog, happy you are. You jump and eat and say "Cua, cua."

❄ ❄ ❄ ❄ ❄

This is like the English rhyme "Ladybug, Ladybug."

Cigüeña, pateña, *tu casita se te quema;* *tus hijitos se te van* *a la raya Portugal;* *mándales una cartita* *y ellos volverán.*	Stork, long legs, your little house is burning, your children are leaving for the Portuguese border; send them a letter and they will return.

From *The Instructor*, F. A. Owen Publishing Company, Danville, New York; February, 1965, page 129. Reprinted by permission.

FORMULILLAS PARA "EL QUEDO"

(Formulas for "Counting Off")

1. *En el patio de mi casa*   In the patio of my house
   hay un palo de arroz.   there's a tree of rice.
   Apostemos, apostemos,   Let's bet, let's bet,
   el que queda veintidós.   who'll be 22.
      (The one counted out.)

2. *Pin-uno, pin-dos,*
   pin-tres, pin-cuatro,
   pin-cinco, pin-seis,
   pin-siete, pin-ocho.

3. *Chini mini mani, mo,*   A nonsense counting-off rhyme.
   el chinito, Francisco,
   y con leri, leri, lo,
   chini, mini, mani, mo.

4. *Pim, pim, serapím,*   Another nonsense rhyme.
   agua, ronda, San Miguel,
   Arcángel.

5. *Botón, botón, de la bota*
   botera.
   Chiribitón.
   ¡Fue—ra!   Out!

6. *Una, dona, trena,*
   cadena,
   tumbaca, viraca,
   viro, virón,
   cuéntalos bien   Count them well, for it's now
   que las doce son.   twelve.

7. Counting buttons on a dress:

   Niña, monja, doncella,   Little girl, nun, maiden,
   casada, viuda, olvidada,   married, widowed, forgotten,
   enamorada.   in love.

8. *Una vieja mató un gato* An old lady killed a cat with
con la punta del zapato. the tip of her shoe. The shoe
El zapato se rompió, came apart and the old lady
y la vieja se en-fa-dó. got angry.

(From *Boletín del Folklore Dominicano*, Diciembre 1947, año II, nu. 11, p. 61.)

EL ALFABETO
(The alphabet)

Students like to chant these rhymes in chorus, to learn the correct sound of vowels and consonants.

EL PATIO DE MI CASA

El patio de mi casa es The patio of my house is
muy particular: very special; when it rains
cuando llueve se moja it gets wet just like the others.
igual que los demás.
H - I - J - K
L - Ll - M - A
Que si tú no me quieres If you don't like me, some
otro amigo me querrá. other friend will like me.
H - I - J - K
L - Ll - M - O
Que si tú no me quieres If you don't like me, I'll get
otro amigo tendré yo. another friend.

❀   ❀   ❀   ❀   ❀

A - B - C - D
La burra se me fue The burro ran away from me
por la calle de tía Merced. down Aunt Merced's street.

❀   ❀   ❀   ❀   ❀

a - e - i - o - u
El burro sabe más que tú. The donkey knows more than
you.

✿ ✿ ✿ ✿ ✿

A - E - I - O - U
Arbolito del Perú.   Little tree of Peru.
Yo tengo nueve años.   I am nine years old.
¿Cuántos años tienes tú?   How old are you?

✿ ✿ ✿ ✿ ✿

A - E - I - O - U
Yo me llamo María.   My name is María.
¿Cómo te llamas tú?   What's your name?

LAS CUENTAS
(Counting)

These verses can help to teach numbers to students.

1.

Uno, dos, tres, cuatro,	
cinco,	1, 2, 3, 4, 5,
cinco, cuatro, tres, dos,	
uno;	5, 4, 3, 2, 1;
siete y siete son catorce,	7 and 7 are 14,
tres por siete veintiuno;	3 times 7 are 21.
en Veracruz sale el sol y	In Veracruz the sun comes out,
en Acapulco, la luna.	and in Acapulco, the moon.

2.

Yo soy el farolero	I am the lamplighter of the
de la puerta del Sol;	gate of the Sun;
subo la escalera	I climb the ladder and light
y enciendo el farol;	the lamp;
luego que lo enciendo,	When I light it,
me pongo a cantar;	I begin to sing:
dos y dos son cuatro,	2 and 2 are 4,
cuatro y dos son seis,	4 and 2 are 6
seis y dos son ocho,	6 and 2 are 8

ocho y ocho, dieciséis,	8 and 8, 16
y ocho, veinticuatro,	and 8, 24,
y ocho, treinta y dos,	and 8, 32,
más diez que añado,	plus ten that I add,
son cuarenta y dos.	makes 42.
Dos y dos son cuatro,	2 and 2 are 4,
tres y tres son seis;	3 and 3 are 6,
seis y dos son ocho,	6 and 2 are 8,
y ocho dieciséis.	and 8, 16.
Trala lala lala, trala lala la.	
Sin equivocarme, yo ya	Without making a mistake, now
sé sumar.	I know how to add.
Dos por dos son cuatro,	2 times 2 are 4,
dos por cinco diez;	2 times 5 are 10;
seis por cinco treinta,	6 times 5, 30,
diez por diez cien.	10 times 10, 100.
Trala lala lala, trala lala la.	
Ya voy aprendiendo	Now I'm learning to multiply.
a multiplicar.	
Oye, farolero, prende	Listen, lamplighter, light
mi farol;	my lamp;
ya hace mucho tiempo que	for a long time ago the sun set.
se puso el sol.	
Trala lala lala, trala lala la.	

From *El Cancionero de la Escuela y del Hogar,* by Leonardo Lis, Editorial Progreso, Mexico, D.F., Mexico, page 15. Permission to reprint granted by publisher.

3. This rhyme is used for counting while jumping rope.

Cinco, diez, quince,	
veinte.	5, 10, 15, 20.
Ya el agua está caliente.	Now the water is hot.

V Songs and Singing Games

CANTANDO CONTANDO

(Singing While Counting)

Up the scale:

Uno - dos - tres - cuatro - cinco - seis - siete - ocho.

Down the scale, counting backwards:

Ocho - siete - seis - cinco - cuatro - tres - dos - uno.

To the tune of "Here We Go Loopty Loo" or "The Bear Went Over the Mountain":

Uno - dos - y tres - cuatro - cinco - y seis - siete - ocho - nueve - diez - once - doce.

VAMOS A APLAUDIR

(Let's Clap)

All form a circle and to the tune of "Here We Go 'Round the Mulberry Bush", sing the following words and applaud:

Vamos a aplaudir,
vamos a aplaudir,
vamos a aplaudir.
(Clap, clap, clap, clap, clap in rhythm, at the same time singing.)
La-la-la-la-la.

Or, to the same tune, each child takes a turn indicating the parts of the body as he sings:

Cabeza, pies, dedos,	Head, feet, fingers . . .
cabeza, pies, dedos,	
cabeza, pies, dedos,	
(All together) *Vamos a aplaudir.*	

All children clap as each one sings the verse in turn.

TOCA LA CAMPANA

(Ring the Bell)

To the tune of "Frere Jacques."

Martinillo, Martinillo,	Little Martin, little Martin,
¿duermes tú, duermes tú?	are you sleeping? etc.
Toca la campana,	Ring the bell, etc.
toca la campana.	
Tin, tan, ton, tin, tan, ton.	Ding, dang, dong, etc.

LOS INDITOS
(Ten Little Indians)

Uno, dos y tres inditos,
cuatro, cinco, seis inditos,
siete, ocho, nueve inditos—
diez inditos son.

Diez, nueve, ocho inditos,
siete, seis, cinco inditos,
cuatro, tres y dos inditos—
un indito hay.

LA ROPA
(Clothing)

To the tune of "The Bear Went Over the Mountain," this song can be used to teach young children the names of articles of clothing.

Estos son mis zapatos,   (Point to shoes.)
éstos son mis zapatos,
éstos son mis zapatos,
tra-la-la-la-la-la.

Este es mi sombrero,   (Point to hat.)
éste es mi sombrero,
éste es mi sombrero,
tra-la-la-la-la-la.

Esta es mi faldita,   (Girls point to skirts.)
ésta es mi faldita,
ésta es mi faldita,
tra-la-la-la-la-la.

Esta es mi blusa,   (Girls point to blouses.)
ésta es mi blusa,
ésta es mi blusa,
tra-la-la-la-la-la.

Este es mi vestido, etc.   (Girls point to dresses.)

Estos son pantalones, etc.   (Boys point to trousers.)

Esta es la camisa, etc.   (Boys point to shirts.)

CASCABELES
(Jingle Bells)

Cascabeles, cascabeles,
tra-la-la-la-la.
Qué alegría todo el día,
tra-la-la-la-la.

Jingle bells, jingle bells,
tra-la-la-la-la.
What fun all the day,
tra-la-la-la-la.

¿A DONDE SE FUE MI PERRITO?
(Where Has My Little Dog Gone?)

¿A dónde, a dónde se fue mi perrito?
¿A dónde, a dónde se fue?
Con orejas largas y cola cortada.
¿A dónde, a dónde se fue?

MI CONEJITO CORRE ASI
(My Little Rabbit Runs Like This)

To the tune of "Merrily We Roll Along."

Mi conejito corre así,
corre así, corre así,
mi conejito corre así,
la-la-la-la-la-la.

My little rabbit runs like this,
runs like this, etc.

TE VEO, TE VEO

(I see you, I see you)

The children form two lines, back to back. They turn their heads, each looking at the one behind him, as they sing:

Te veo, te veo.   (They turn completely around
La-la-la-la-la-la.   and clap hands, face to face.)

Te veo, te veo.
La-la-la-la-la-la.

Tú me ves y yo te veo,   You see me and I see you, then
   luego tú me ves a mí.   you see me.
Yo te miro, tú me miras,   I look at you, you look at me,
   luego yo te miro a ti.   then I look at you.
(They make gestures of looking at each other.)

Te veo, te veo,   (Turn completely around, and
la-la-la-la-la-la.   clap hands, face to face.)
Te veo, te veo,
la-la-la-la-la-la.

Tú me ves y yo te veo.   You see me and I see you.
Si me pillas correré.   If you catch me I will run.
Yo te miro, tú me miras,   I look at you, you look at me.
   si me pillas correré.   If you catch me I will run.

(Upon saying "If you catch me . . ." the children run in rhythm, still keeping in their lines.)

From *Billiken*, Editorial Atlantida, S.A., Buenos Aires, Argentina, January 18, 1965. Permission to reprint granted by the publishers.

Te veo, te veo

por Elisa Gayan

Alegre

Te ve - o, te ve - o, la la la la la la. Te ve - o, te ve - o, la la la la la la.

Tú me ves y yo te ve - o, lue-go tú me ves a mí. Yo te mi-ro, tú me mi-ras lue-go, yo te mi-ro a ti.

LOS COLORES

(The colors)

The whole class may play.

Needed: Eight pieces of colored paper, all different.

Eight children stand in front of the class. The Leader gives each one of the pieces of colored paper and whispers the name of the color it represents to each one. She then walks behind them and touches one on the back so that the rest of the class cannot see who is tagged. As she is doing this, the class sings:

Los colores brillan, rojo,	The colors shine, red, white
blanco y amarillo.	and yellow.
Otros son más suaves,	Others are more soft, green,
verde, negro y azul . . .	black, and blue.

The rest of the class now takes turns guessing which color was tagged. They may say: *"¿Es verde?"* and the child in front who represents *verde,* must reply, *"Sí, es verde,"* or *"No, no es verde."* When someone has guessed the correct color, the song is sung again and another color is chosen.

From *Saludos Amigos,* Beginner's Spanish, Teacher's Manual, page 20, KQED Instructional Television Service, San Francisco, page 20. Permission to reprint granted by Dr. Manuel Guerra.

Los colores

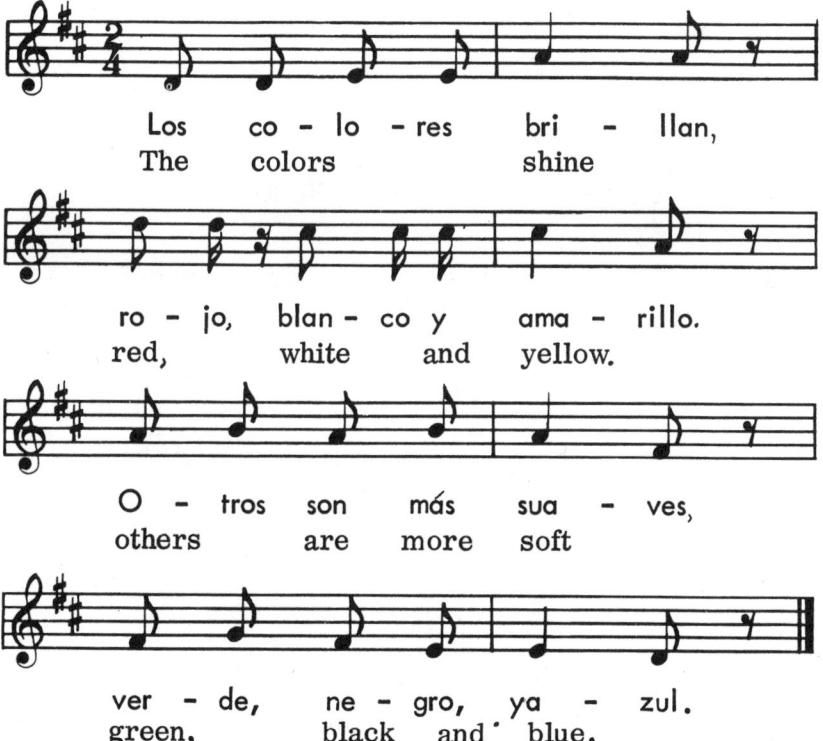

Los   co - lo - res   bri - llan,
The   colors   shine

ro - jo,   blan - co y   ama - rillo.
red,   white   and   yellow.

O - tros   son   más   sua - ves,
others   are   more   soft

ver - de,   ne - gro,   ya - zul.
green,   black and blue.

EL JUEGO CHIRIMBOLO

(The Chirimbolo Game)

Any number may play.

Players begin singing in a circle:

El juego chirimbolo, *¡qué bonito es!*	The chirimbolo game, how pretty it is!

They drop hands and go through the movements indicated by the words, facing toward the center:

Con un pie, otro pie, *una mano, otra mano,* *un codo, otro codo,* *el juego chirimbolo,* *¡qué bonito es!*	With one foot, another foot, one hand, another hand, one elbow, another elbow. . . .

From *Mi Libro*, Gessler Publishing Company, New York, page 21. Permission to reprint granted by publishers.

El juego chirimbolo

(Canción con algunos movimientos)

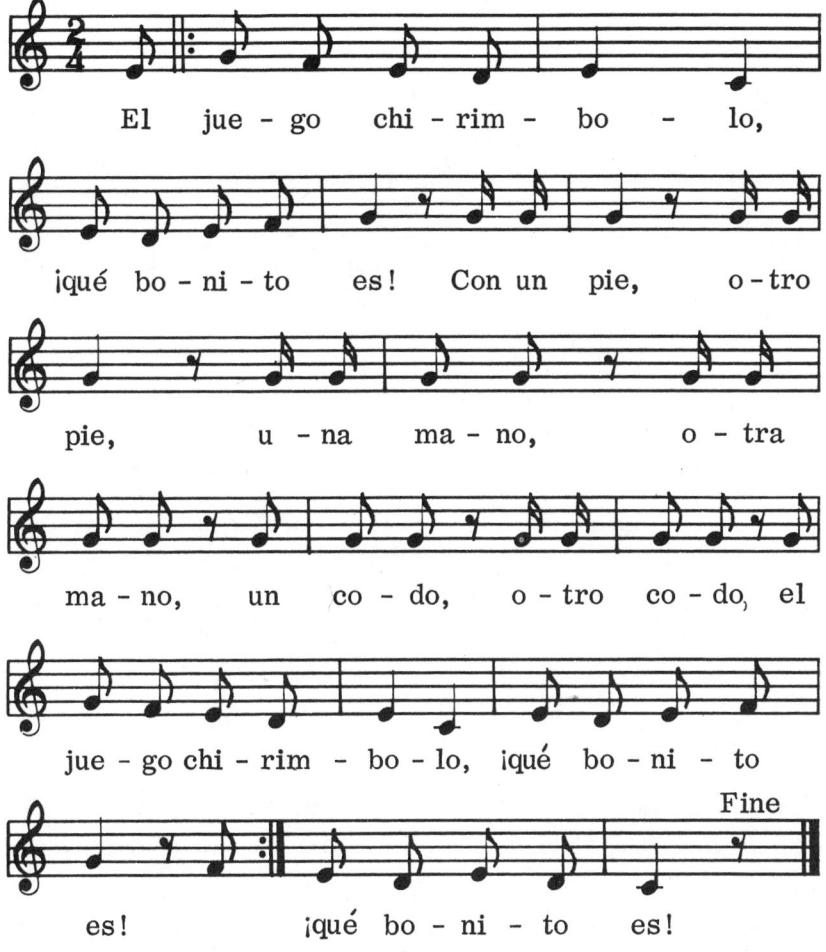

El jue - go chi - rim - bo - lo,

¡qué bo - ni - to es! Con un pie, o - tro

pie, u - na ma - no, o - tra

ma - no, un co - do, o - tro co - do, el

jue - go chi - rim - bo - lo, ¡qué bo - ni - to

Fine

es! ¡qué bo - ni - to es!

NARANJA DULCE, LIMON PARTIDO

(Sweet Orange, Cut Lemon)

About 30 may play this game, usually played by girls, and said to have originated in Costa Rica.

Players form a circle with one person in the center. As they walk around they sing:

Naranja dulce,	Sweet orange,
limón partido,	cut lemon,
dame un abrazo	give me an embrace,
que yo te pido.	I beg you.
Si fueran falsos	If my vows
mis juramentos,	were untrue,
en otros tiempos	in time
se olvidarán.	they will be forgotten.

The one in the center sings:

Toca la marcha,	Play the march,
mi pecho llora:	my heart is crying;
Adiós, señora,	Goodbye, señora,
yo ya me voy.	I'm going now.

When the singing is ended, the one in the center goes to someone in the circle, gives her an *abrazo* and they exchange places as the game continues.

Naranja dulce, limón partido

Na -ran-ja dul - ce, li - món par -

ti - do, da-me un a - bra - zo que yo te

pi - do. Si fue - ran fal - sos mis ju - ra -

men - tos, en o - tros tiem - pos se ol-vi - da -

rán. To - ca la mar - cha, mi pe - cho

llo - ra. A - diós, se - ño - ra, yo ya me voy.

ARROZ CON LECHE
(Rice With Milk)

In Venezuela this game is often called *"Arroz con coco"* (Rice with coconut). The version below is played by children of Costa Rica.

Children take hands and form a circle. One child stands in the center. As children walk around they sing:

Arroz con leche,	Rice with milk,
me quiero casar	I want to marry
con una viudita	a little widow
de la capital.	from the Capital.
Que sepa coser,	One who can sew,
que sepa bordar,	who can embroider,
que ponga la mesa	who can set the table
en su santo lugar.	in its holy place.

The child in the center now sings:

Yo soy la viudita,	I am the little widow,
la hija del Rey,	daughter of the King,
que quiero casarme	who wants to marry,
y no hallo con quien.	but can't find anyone to marry.

The other children sing:

Pues, cásate, niña,	Well, marry, my girl,
que yo te daré	and I will give you
zapatos y medias	shoes and stockings,
color de café.	brown in color.

The one in the center points to someone in the circle as she sings each of the following lines:

Contigo, sí,	You I will marry,
contigo, no,	you I won't marry,
contigo, mi vida,	you, my darling,
me casaré yo.	I will marry.

When she reaches the last line, the one she points to as she says the word *yo* now becomes the *viudita* in the center as the game continues as before.

Arroz con leche
(Rice With Milk)

SAN SERENI

A traditional singing game of Puerto Rico which 30 or 35 may play.

A circle is formed with one person in the center. The other players walk around, singing:

San Sereni de la buena,	Saint Sereni of the good life.
buena vida,	
Hacen así, así, los	
zapateros así.	Shoemakers do it like this.
Así, así, así me gusta a mí.	Like this is the way I like it.

The player in the center imitates the movements of a shoe-maker as they sing. Another player then takes his place in the center as the circle walks around, singing:

San Sereni de la buena, buena vida,	
hacen así, así, así, los	
carpinteros así.	. . . carpenters . . .
Así, así, así me gusta a mí.	

This time the one in the center imitates the movements of a carpenter. The same verse is sung again several more times, using the words *lavanderas* (laundresses), *jardineros* (gardeners), *panaderos* (bakers), *sombrereros* (hatmakers), *carniceros* (butchers), etc. With each new verse, the player in the center imitates the movements of the worker named.

Another way to play the game is to have a circle of players without one in the center. The circle sings the first line as they walk around, then all pause and go through the motions of the worker as they sing the rest of the verse.

San Sereni

San Se - re - ní   de la   bue - na, bue - na

vi - da, ha - cen a - sí, a -

sí, los za - pa - te - ros a - sí. A - sí, a -

sí, a - sí me gus - tan a mí.

MI GATITO

(My Kitten)

Yo tengo un gato, un gatito;	I have a cat, a little cat;
es lindo mi gato, mi gatito;	my cat, my little cat is pretty;
si él tiene hambre, mi gatito,	if he is hungry, my little cat
abre la boca y dice: Oh,	opens his mouth and says: Oh,
miau, miau, miau, miau.	meow, meow, meow, meow.

Mi gatito

Yo ten-go un ga-to, un ga-ti-to; es

lin-do mi ga-to, mi ga - ti - to; si

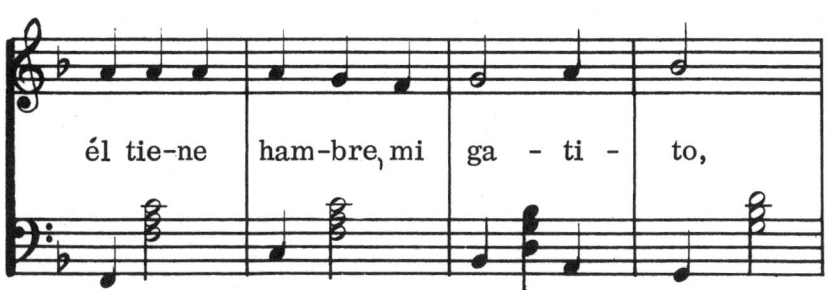

From *Beginning Lessons for Teaching Spanish to Small Children,* by Elizabeth L. Etnire, Division of Field Services, Central Michigan College, Mt. Pleasant, Michigan. Reprinted by permission of the author.

ME REGALARON UN VIOLIN

(They Gave me a Violin)

Para el día de mi santo	For my birthday
me regalaron un violín.	they gave me a violin.
Yi-ri-yin-yin, el violín,	
yi-ri-yi-yin, el violín.	·
Ay, qué dichosa yo me	
quedé.	Oh, how happy it made me.
Ay, qué dichosa yo me quedé.	
Para el día de mi santo	
me regalaron un tambor.	. . . a drum.
Para-pon-pon, el tambor,	
Para-pon-pon, el tambor.	
Ay, qué contenta yo me quedé.	
Ay, qué contenta yo me quedé.	

From *Saludos Amigos,* Beginner's Spanish, Teacher's Manual, KQED Instructional Television Service, San Francisco, page 23. Permission to reprint granted by Dr. Manuel Guerra.

Me regalaron un violín

MI CHACRA

(My Farm)

Vengan a ver mi chacra,	Come and see my farm,
que es hermosa.	for it is lovely.
Vengan a ver mi chacra,	
que es hermosa.	
El pollito hace así:	The chick goes this way:
ki-ki-ri.	
El pollito hace así:	
ki-ki-ri.	
O pas, camarade,	(French: "Walk in step,"
o pas, camarade,	pronounced: O pah,
o pas, o pas, o pas;	cah-mah-rahd.)
o pas, camarade, o pas camarade,	
o pas, o pas, o pas.	

Continue with:

2. *El perrito hace así:*   The dog goes like this:
   guau-guau.   bow-wow.
3. *El gato hace así: mi-au.*   The cat goes like this: me-ow.
4. *El burrito hace así: ji-jo.*   The burro . . . hee-haw.
5. *El patito hace así:*
   cua-cua.   The duck . . . quack-quack.
6. *El chanchito hace así:*
   oinc-oinc.   The pig . . . oink-oink.

From *Amigos Cantando,* Cooperative Recreation Service, Delaware, Ohio, page 18. Permission to reprint granted by the publishers.

My Farm

Mi chacra

Trans. by Olcutt and Phyllis Sanders   Argentine Folk Song

Come, come and see my farm for it   is love-ly.
Ven - gan a ver mi cha-cra que_es her - mo -sa.

Come, come and see my farm for it   is love - ly.
Ven - gan a ver mi cha-cra que_es her-mo-sa.

El po-lli-to goes like this: kee-kee-ree; El po-
El po-lli-to ha - ce_a-sí: ki - ki - ri. El po -

lli- to goes like this: kee-kee-ree. O pas, ca-ma-rade,
lli-to ha - ce_a-sí: ki - ki - ri.

O pas, ca-ma-rade, o pas, o pas, o pas;   o

pas, ca-ma-rade, o pas, ca-ma-rade, o pas, o pas, o pas.

PERICA
(Parrot)

Cuando la perica quiere
que el perico vaya a misa,
se levanta bien temprano
y le plancha la camisa.

When Perica wishes
her husband to go to mass,
she rises very early
and irons his shirt.

Refrain:
Ay, mi perica, dame la pata
Para ponerte las alpargatas.

Oh, Perica, give me your foot,
so I may put on your sandals.

Cuando la perica quiere
que el perico coma arroz,
le salcocha la comida
y se la comen los dos.

When Perica wishes
her husband to eat rice,
she parboils the meal
and they both eat it.

Refrain: *Ay, mi perica, . . .*

Cuando la perica quiere
que el perico se enamore,
se quita las plumas viejas
y se viste de colores.

When Perica wishes
her husband to love her,
she takes off her old feathers
and dresses in bright colors.

Perica

Trans. by Olcutt Sanders   Chilean Folk Song

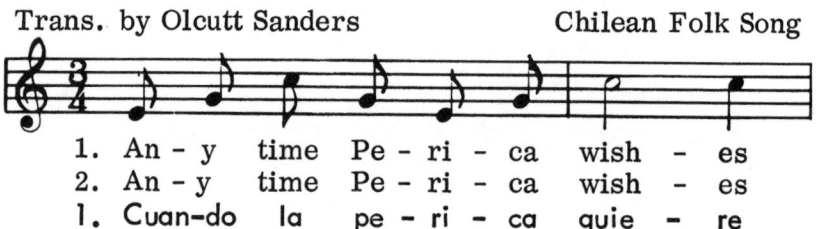

1. An - y   time   Pe - ri - ca   wish - es
2. An - y   time   Pe - ri - ca   wish - es
1. Cuan-do   la   pe - ri - ca   quie - re

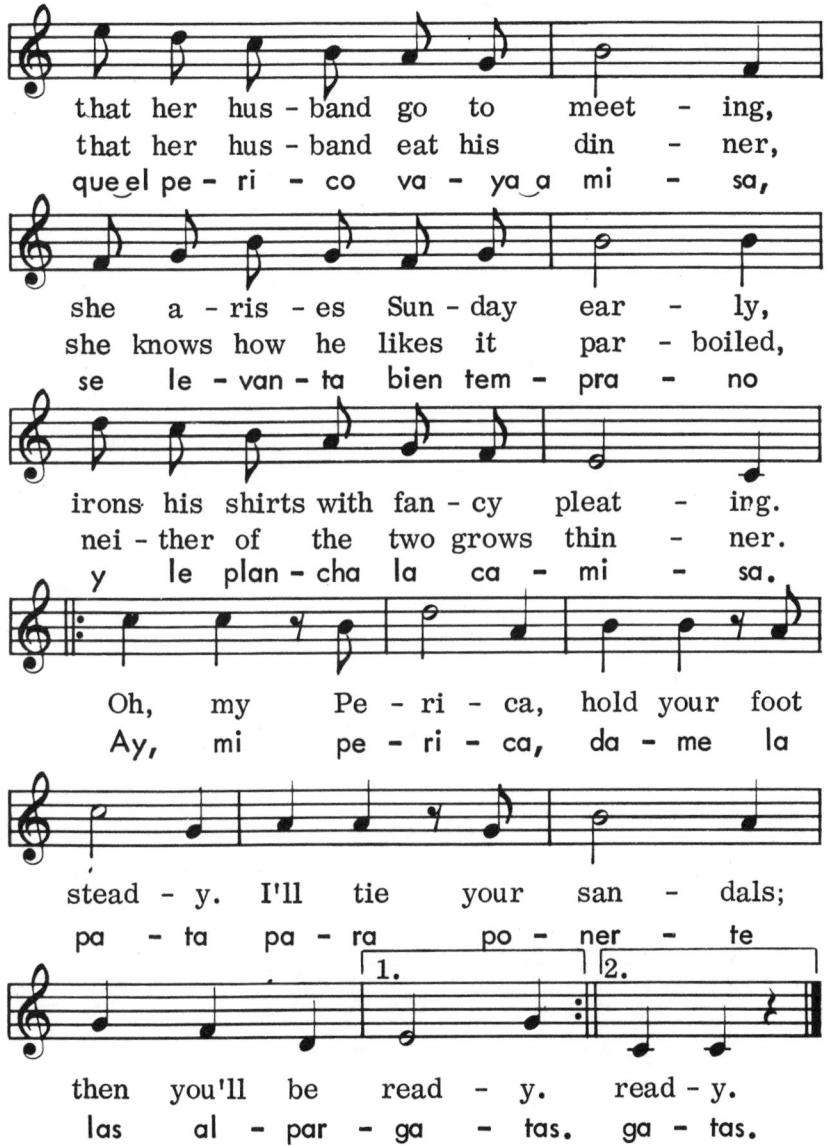

From *Amigos Cantando,* Cooperative Recreation Service, Delaware, Ohio, page 5.
Permission to reprint granted by the publishers.

YO ME VOY
(I am leaving)

Yo me voy, yo me voy,	I am leaving, I am leaving,
cuando a mí me dé la gana.	whenever I please.
Yo me vine por un día	I came for a day
y me estuve una semana.	and I have been here a week.

Yo me voy

From *Folk Songs and Stories of the Americas,* Pan American Union, Washington, D. C. Permission to reprint granted by the Music Division, Pan American Union.

VAPORES Y TAMBORES
(Boats and Drums)

¡Qué bonito que corre el mar	How beautiful is the sea
debajo de los vapores!	beneath the boats.
Sirena, morena,	Oh, my dark mermaid,
repícame los tambores.	beat the drums for me.

Vapores y tambores

¡Qué bo - ni - to   que corre el   mar   de -

ba-jo   de los   va - po - res! Si - re - na, mo-

re - na,   re - pí - ca-me los tam - bo - res.

From *Folk Songs and Stories of the Americas,* Pan American Union, Washington, D. C. Permission to reprint granted by the Music Division, Pan American Union.

A LAS PUERTAS DEL CIELO
(At the Doors of Heaven)

A las puertas del cielo	At the doors of Heaven
venden zapatos	they sell shoes
para los angelitos	for the little angels
que están descalzos.	who are barefoot.

Refrain:

Duérmete, niño,	Sleep, child,
duérmete, niño,	sleep, child,
duérmete, niño,	sleep, child,
do-do, do-do, do-do,	. . .
Ave María, do-do.	

A los niños que duermen	The children who sleep,
Dios bendice;	God will bless.
a las madres que velan	The mothers who watch over
Dios las asiste.	them
	God will attend.

Refrain: . . .

From *Spanish Folk Songs of the Southwest,* collected and transcribed by Mary R. Van Stone, Academy Guild Press, Fresno, California. Permission to reprint granted by the publishers.

A las⹀Puertas del cielo
A Lullaby

EL TORTILLERO

(The Tortilla Vender)

Noche oscura, nada veo. — Dark night, I see nothing,
Pero llevo mi farol; — But I carry my lantern.
por tus puertas voy pasando, — I am passing by your doors
y cantando con amor. — and singing with love.

Refrain:
Mas, voy cantando — But I am singing
con harta pena. — with great pain.
¿Quién compra mis tortillas? — Who will buy my tortillas?
¡Tortillas buenas! — Good tortillas!

Bella ingrata, no respondes — Ungrateful, you do not reply
a mi grito piacentero. — to my begging cry.
Cuando pasa por tu casa — When the tortilla vender
pregonando el tortillero. — shouts his wares by your house.

(Refrain)

Ya me voy a retirar con — Now I will leave with
mi canasta y farol, — my basket and lantern,
sin tener tu compasión — without your taking pity
de este pobre tortillero. — on this poor tortilla vender.

(Refrain)

From *Amigos Cantando,* Cooperative Recreation Service, Delaware, Ohio, page 24.
Permission to reprint granted by the publishers.

The Tortilla Vender
El tortillero

Trans. by Olcutt Sanders

Chilean Folk Song

Thru the   dark-ness   now I   wan-der
No-che o-scu - ra,   na - da ve - o.

With a lan - tern for my light. _____
Pe - ro lle - vo mi fa - rol; _____

_____ Past your door-way I am go - ing;
_____ Por tus puer - tas voy pa - san - do,

So I'll sing a fond good-night. _____
y can - tan - do con a - mor. _____

Refrain:

Now _____ with deep sad - ness _____
Mas, _____ voy can - tan - do _____

My _____ wares I cry them. ___ Who'll
con _____ har - ta pe - na. ___ ¿Quién

buy my good___ to - sta - i - tas? _____
com-pra mis ___ to - sta - i - tas? _____

1.   2.

Tor - ti-llas! Buy them! Buy them!
Tor - ti - llas bue - nas? bue - nas?

RIQUI RAN

Aserrín, aserrán,	Aserrin, aserran,
los maderos de San Juan	All the woodsmen of San Juan
comen queso, comen pan.	eat cheese and bread;
Los de Rique, alfeñique;	those from Rique, sugar candy,
los de Roque, alfondoque,	those from Roque, loaf sugar,
ri-qui, ri-que, ri-qui, ran.	ri-qui, ri-que, ri-qui, ran.
Aserrín, aserrán,	Aserrin, aserran,
las abejas vienen, van;	the bees come and go;
miel laboran para el pan,	gather honey for their bread,
liban flores las de Rique,	those from Rique sip flowers,
cual almíbar de alfeñique,	like nectar of sugar candy,
y el panal de las de Roque	and the honey combs of Roque
se parece a un alfondoque,	are like a piece of loaf sugar,
ri-qui, ri-que, ri-qui, ran.	ri-qui, etc. . . .
Aserrín aserrán,	Aserrin, aserran,
los chiquillos, ¿dónde están?	Where are all the children?
Todos a dormir se van.	All have gone to sleep,
Soñarán con alfeñique	to dream of white sugar candy
como sueñan los de Rique,	like those of Rique,
y mañana un alfondoque	and tomorrow a loaf sugar,
comerán con los de Roque,	they will eat with those from
ri-qui, ri-que, ri-qui, ran.	Roque,
	ri-qui, etc. . . .

From *Amigos Cantado*, Cooperative Recreation Service, Delaware, Ohio, page 13. Permission to reprint granted by the publishers.

Riqui ran

Trans. by Olcutt Sanders   Latin-American Folk Song

A-se - rrín,   a - se - rrán,   All   the
A-se - rrín,   a - se - rrán,   los   ma -

woods-men   of   San   Juan   eat   their
de - ros   de   San   Juan   co - men

cheese and eat their   pan. Those from   Ri-que al-fe-
que - so, co - men   pan.   Los de   Ri - que, al-fe-

ñi - que; those   from   Ro - que,   al - fon -
ñi - que; los   de   Ro - que,   al - fon -

do - que,   ri - qui,   ri - que, ri - qui   ran.
do - que,   ri - qui,   ri - que, ri - qui   ran.

TECOLOTE

(The owl)

Tecolote, ¿dónde viene?	Where do you come from owl?
Tecolote, ¿dónde viene?	
Yo vengo de Colorado,	I come from Colorado . . .
yo vengo de Colorado.	
Ay. Cu-cu-rru, cu, cu, cu,	
cu-cu-rru, cu, cu, cu,	
pobrecito animalito	poor little animal
tiene hambre,	is hungry, little owl. Oh.
Tecolotito, ay.	
Vengo a traerte una noticia,	I bring you news . . .
vengo a traerte una noticia,	
que tu amor ya es perdido,	That your love is lost . . .
que tu amor ya es perdido.	
Ay. Cu-cu-rru, cu, cu, cu,	
cu-cu-rru, cu, cu, cu,	
pobrecito animalito	
tiene hambre,	
Tecolotito, ay.	

Tecolote

cu, cu-rru, cu, cu, cu, po-bre-ci - to

an-i - ma-li-to. tie-ne ham-bre, Te-co-lo-ti - to. Ay.

From *Spanish Folk Songs of the Southwest*, collected and transcribed by Mary R. Van Stone, Academy Guild Press, Fresno, California. Permission to reprint granted by the publishers.

NTC SPANISH TEXTS AND MATERIALS

Computer Software
Basic Vocabulary Builder on Computer
Amigo: Vocabulary Software

Videocassette, Activity Book, and Instructor's Manual
VideoPasaporte Español

Graded Readers
Diálogos simpáticos
Cuentitos simpáticos
Cuentos simpáticos
Beginner's Spanish Reader
Easy Spanish Reader

Workbooks
Así escribimos
Ya escribimos
¡A escribir!
Composiciones ilustradas
Spanish Verb Drills

Exploratory Language Books
Spanish for Beginners
Let's Learn Spanish Picture Dictionary
Spanish Picture Dictionary
Getting Started in Spanish
Just Enough Spanish

Conversation Books
¡Empecemos a charlar!
Basic Spanish Conversation
Everyday Conversations in Spanish

Manual and Audiocassette
How to Pronounce Spanish Correctly

Text and Audiocassette Learning Packages
Just Listen 'n Learn Spanish
Just Listen 'n Learn Spanish Plus
Practice and Improve Your Spanish
Practice and Improve Your Spanish Plus

High-Interest Readers
Sr. Pepino Series
    La momia desaparece
    La casa embrujada
    El secuestro

Journeys to Adventure Series
    Un verano misterioso
    La herencia
    El ojo de agua
    El enredo
    El jaguar curioso

Humor in Spanish and English
Spanish à la Cartoon

Puzzle and Word Game Books
Easy Spanish Crossword Puzzles
Easy Spanish Word Games & Puzzles
Easy Spanish Vocabulary Puzzles

Transparencies
Everyday Situations in Spanish

Black-line Masters
Spanish Verbs and Vocabulary Bingo Games
Spanish Crossword Puzzles
Spanish Culture Puzzles
Spanish Word Games
Spanish Vocabulary Puzzles

Handbooks and Reference Books
Complete Handbook of Spanish Verbs
Spanish Verbs and Essentials of Grammar
Nice 'n Easy Spanish Grammar
Tratado de ortografía razonada
Redacte mejor comercialmente
Guide to Correspondence in Spanish
Guide to Spanish Idioms

Dictionaries
Vox Modern Spanish and English Dictionary
Vox New College Spanish and English Dictionary
Vox Compact Spanish and English Dictionary
Vox Everyday Spanish and English Dictionary
Vox Traveler's Spanish and English Dictionary
Vox Super-Mini Spanish and English Dictionary
Cervantes-Walls Spanish and English Dictionary

For further information or a current catalog, write:
National Textbook Company
a division of *NTC Publishing Group*
4255 West Touhy Avenue
Lincolnwood, Illinois 60646-1975 U.S.A.